8.94 Fulin 469

Today
IN AMERICAN DRAMA

Today
IN AMERICAN DRAMA

✤

FRANK HURBURT O'HARA

GREENWOOD PRESS, PUBLISHERS
NEW YORK

ACKNOWLEDGMENTS

JUST AS A PLAY CANNOT REALLY COME INTO BEING without the various and important departments of production, each of them forwarding the interpretation of what the playwright means to say, so of course a book about plays cannot be written without a great deal of assistance, and a list of those who have helped in the process looks like the list of acknowledgments printed in small type at the end of a theater program. This preliminary word merely reverses the program practice, placing the thank-you's first and in larger type.

Many writers, actors, critics, scholars, publishers, and producers have helped, directly or indirectly, in the making of these discussions, which simply aim to set up some of our more recent American drama against the old labels which not so long ago were very easy academic gestures. A sort of blanket appreciation is herewith expressed to individuals, genuinely if tersely; and for the direct quotations which will be found rather generously distributed throughout this book, specific acknowledgments are cordially made.

v

ACKNOWLEDGMENTS

Thus, the quotations of Eugene O'Neill's views upon tragedy and upon aspects of *Anna Christie* and *The Hairy Ape* are reprinted through the courtesy of Barrett H. Clark and are from his book, *Eugene O'Neill, the Man and His Plays,* published by Robert M. McBride & Company, New York; revised edition, 1936.

Quotations from recent plays are to be credited as follows:

From *Winterset* and *Knickerbocker Holiday,* by Maxwell Anderson, reprinted by permission of Anderson House, Washington, D.C.

From *The Philadelphia Story,* by Philip Barry, reprinted by permission of Mr. Barry.

From *No Time for Comedy,* by S. N. Behrman, reprinted by permission of Random House, Inc., New York.

From *Family Portrait,* by Lenore Coffee and William Joyce Cowen, reprinted by permission of Random House, Inc., New York.

From *What a Life,* by Clifford Goldsmith, reprinted by permission of Mr. Goldsmith and of Brandt and Brandt Dramatic Department, Inc., New York. Copyright, 1938, by Clifford Goldsmith. All rights reserved.

From *Johnny Johnson,* by Paul Green, reprinted by permission of Samuel French, New York, publishers.

ACKNOWLEDGMENTS

by permission of Longmans, Green & Co., New York, publishers.

From *Bury the Dead* and *The Gentle People*, by Irwin Shaw, reprinted by permission of Random House, Inc., New York.

From *Boy Meets Girl*, by Samuel and Bella Spewack, reprinted by permission of Random House, Inc., New York.

From *Of Mice and Men*, by John Steinbeck, copyright, 1937, reprinted by permission of The Viking Press, Inc., New York.

From *Daughters of Atreus*, by Robert Turney, reprinted by permission of and special arrangement with Alfred A. Knopf, Inc., New York, authorized publishers.

It is always to be hoped that, reading about plays, one may be prompted to proceed to the reading of the full play, or to seeing the play in production, or —best of all—to doing both.

Acknowledgment should be made, and with particular appreciation, to my sometime collaborator, Mrs. Margueritte Harmon Bro, who has managed to find time from her activities as writer and lecturer to give material assistance in the preparation of TODAY IN AMERICAN DRAMA.

F.H.O'H.

THE UNIVERSITY OF CHICAGO
October 1939

TODAY IN AMERICAN DRAMA:

I.

TRAGEDIES WITHOUT FINALITY

IF ANYONE IS GOING TO BE BOLD ENOUGH TO CLASSIFY plays at all today, he might as well say at the very beginning that terms like "tragedy," "comedy," "farce" and "melodrama" are after all only labels academically pasted onto stories which creative writers contrive for the stage because they have a story they must tell. The story is the thing, as every audience knows and every actor knows and certainly every playwright ought to know. Probably there never was a playwright—at least not one whose name lingers in the annals of the stage—who said to himself, "Today, I think I shall write a tragedy." If he were really born to the purple, he had a story to tell and he told it in the most moving way he could tell it because it was that kind of story. If its proportions were heroic and its characters moved with finality toward inevitable catastrophe and the mood of grandeur overshadowed the fact of defeat, then his story was a tragedy. It just happened so.

1

And the category very likely concerned him not at all. Certainly not while he was giving birth to the story.

Since "tragedy" is merely a classifying word which can be used for purposes of discussion, it seems needless to pause too long with those who say, "Tragedy has largely passed from our stage today." Tragedy cannot pass from the American stage, or any other stage, as long as we have human beings caught in a chain of events beyond their control, as long as chance and accident and unpredictable circumstance cry halt to an individual who cannot stop. Nor as long as we have creative artists. For creative artists are much alike in each generation. No doubt if we could gather them together, these playwrights of the centuries, in some great timeless *now* where everything that has happened is still happening, it would make little difference to Euripides if he found himself in the stokehole of a steamship, or to O'Neill if he stood on the battlements of Troy. Each would sense the story around him and begin to give it life upon some stage. The accouterments of the age do not matter a great deal. Shakespeare over and over again wrote the timely thing for the Elizabethan audience, and yet we say easily today, "Shakespeare was of all time." Only the historian or the scholar can point out the timely qualities in a Shakespeare play; almost all of us are aware of the timelessness. Perhaps no playwright more sharply indicated the thinking of his day than Ibsen; today many of his audacities are bromides. The poetic reach of the story of *Peer Gynt* is as vital as it was in the sixties, while only a close student of the Scandinavia of that day could possibly understand the play's local symbolism and political allusions, most of which are surgically stripped from the text before present-day production.

The important thing for the playwright is being able to create a story upon a stage. And even so, he is probably the last to mention its importance unless someone interrupts him at his work or he has to make an after-dinner speech. Most of the time he is preoccupied with the task at hand, or the task is preoccupied with him. Let those come after to analyze his work or himself, if they are stimulated in so doing. Probably it is only rarely that analysis helps the creative process, except as a genuine teacher may occasionally "remind" the growing playwright of something deep within himself which his hand has not quite caught.

But unimportant though the classifying terms may be to the playwright while he is creating, they are convenient words for the rest of us when we are talking about plays. Like all classifying words, they are short cuts. They tell us at least what not to look for. They set the mood of our expectancy. When we see "tragedy," for instance, we do not look for laughter, except perhaps incidentally in the relief which used to be called "comic." We do not look for plot and contrivance for their own sakes. We look for characters who matter vitally because they have willed to do something which they cannot do without wrecking the structure of their souls, or characters whose integrity can make no compromise with circumstances no matter how relentlessly the circumstances batter at the citadel of self. In other words, we look for characters who realize in full measure some of the qualities of personality, some of the emotions which even in average measure may make or break us. The characters of tragedy always have an element of grandeur; they face inevitable defeat; there is finality in the judgment which awaits them —finality for them, but for us the "lift" which comes whenever we see beyond individual catastrophe to some meaning in the pattern of which our own lives are a part.

However, although the main features of tragedy are characteristic of tragedy in any time, it is also obvious that tragedies have their differences from age to age. And therefore those who say that tragedy has largely passed from the American stage are reaching for a fact not without significance. The materials of tragedy have changed somewhat, and the implications of tragedy have changed. Which is only a way of saying that our point of view has changed. We wrest different meaning from finality, and we call different actions "catastrophic." We have different standards, different sanctions for morality; and ethical sanctions are the backdrop against which tragedies are played.

The contemporary tragedy has earmarks, definite distinguishing traits, which place it in a given period much as the wood-burning boilers of an early engine or the crude bone-saws of early surgery speak of phases in the history of engineering and of medicine. Naturally, they reflect the conceptions and the skills of their day. And the same is true, of course, of all the arts. Our tragedy has undoubtedly gone off the grand scale except as it occasionally utilizes some ancient theme and characters to point some living problem. But then, our life has gone off the grand scale all along the line. And sometimes we rather miss the grand scale; it had an atmosphere of assurance. The statuesque proportions of the divine right of kings must have been very impressive to the casual eye. In government today, there are few kings and queens to wield their scepters, and those monarchs we still have are crowned by common consent of the very common people. This is, of course, exactly as we would have it; yet no matter how hard we believe in democracy, a close-up is somewhat disappointing because all the people are so much like ourselves. Still, we understand ourselves a little better than we understand a king, and so the old-style protagonist of royal prerogatives does not walk our stage today. The gods, the supernatural ultimatum, the human sacrifice, have gone out with chariots and battlements and armor. Why should they concern us, except as we allow the illusion of history to give them verisimilitude? We couldn't start a war now, on the stage or off, to bring Helen back to Greece. We'd yawn and look toward Hollywood. Today we start wars for just as fatuous reasons, but the fatuity is our own convincing brand. The grand gesture of the old school has gone.

Today's tragedy is also marked by a preoccupation with psychological quirks. To be sure, the strange workings of the human mind, driven by emotion which races the engines of reason too fast to let the gears mesh—these things have always fascinated the writers of tragedy. They *are* tragedy. But today we measure "responses" and "reflexes"; we catalogue "psychoses." We use a new technique for getting at motivation. We feel that we are being more honest in utilizing life-size figures instead of the larger-than-life figures of another age, for the average citizen is the scale our scientific instruments were made to fit. It is most important, we say, to know the common man.

Tragedy today is also less likely to reflect a moral judgment; it concerns itself less with a "tragic flaw" in the sense of a giving-way in character for which the individual himself is ultimately responsible. Necessarily it still depicts fatal weakness in character, but the weakness is likely to be the result of circumstances over which the individual has no control— just as he has no control over the ensuing circumstances which issue from the interplay of his character and the events about him. Perhaps the whole of life, says our tragedy in certain moods, is just a vast miscasting of parts by a director who is himself an automaton. Perhaps . . . . but only perhaps. We are not sure. Since we lack authentic moral judgment, the punishment meted out by our tragedy today is frequently petty and lifelong instead of tremendous and final. The life of the sinner wears

7

away instead of going out magnificently in one final act of extirpation. Indeed, this loss of finality, this indeterminateness, is the point at which we can most question whether some plays really are tragedies or, instead, the somber serious comedy which also marks the current mood.

All these modifications in tragedy are probably the outgrowth of the one basic factor which has given our age its distinguishing trait: the growth of science. Pure tragedy of the classical mold was doomed when Galileo's telescope projected question marks across a sky which hitherto had been a tapestry of mythology. From that time the stubborn feet of Science moved toward a neutral Nature which needed no placation from, and made no moral demands upon, mankind. The gods retired from the stage. But it wasn't the dramatists who said, "Let there be tragedy without the gods." It wasn't the audiences. It wasn't even the psychologists, although at a casual glance they seem to be the dictators of the stage today. The gods were banished by the "exact" scientists, if we may borrow the term by which the physicists and mathematicians designate themselves. They found out about matter and the laws which appeared to govern it. They found laws for interstellar spaces and laws for the infinitesimal particles called

8

"protons" and "electrons" (words inherited from the Greeks whose gods were no longer useful). Then the biologists began to find laws behind the rest of life and to uncover the whole elaborate theory of evolution.

For a time, even after impersonal mechanism was assumed to operate in all the rest of nature, the supernatural was allowed a dwelling-place in man's mind. Thus the gods, or the Absolute or the Ultimate, whatever the name, could speak to the mind of man; and conscience was a moral arbiter, and *man was responsible for his deeds.* In such a time the implacable moral demands of the older tragedy were still a convincing assumption. But inch by inch the natural laws which operated in the physical world moved in on the mind of man; and the very processes of his thinking and believing and willing and wishing—the whole of his soul—were also explained by laws as "natural" as those which governed the plants and animals and stars. With so many laws of such amazing exactitude it became a Q.E.D. to conclude that all life was operated by invariable laws which needed no gods to account for them.

Not that the average man has ever been too self-consciously aware that it was the perfection and impersonality of the machinery of the universe which

9

was taking away his sense of ultimate responsibility. For one thing, this "average man" is a composite of various points of view not too consistently wrought together, and we are never all of us believing the same thing at the same time. But whatever the beliefs we cling to, we are nevertheless affected by reports emerging with convincing unanimity from the scientist's laboratory. The psychologist, the dramatist, and the common man are forced to face the problem that *if* reality is a mechanism, then morality may be nonsense. If man—any man—is as he is because of ten thousand laws of heredity and environment, then he is not to blame if he fails in life. For after all he is only a spinning top on a spinning earth in a spinning universe for which he is certainly not responsible. Even on the stage, it is not convincing to ask an individual to sacrifice himself for standards which are based upon blind mechanics or cosmic futility. The stage always reflects the general philosophy of the people; and from the beginning, upon the stage or off, conduct has depended upon theory. Man has always tended to square his individual action against the great meridian lines of his universe. In the old days, the gods lent meaning adequate for life's consistent endeavor. The stage did not need to offer comfort when it could offer

10

meaning. In the new day, honest ethics still has to be consistent with reality, and it is clearly difficult to live by ethical compulsions which operate automatically, if at all.

Ours is an age in search of an answer, in search of a standard. Religion? Science? Communism? The New Deal? We lack confidence. So we have plays of questioning or questing, uncertainties or uncertitudes. Even most of the plays of protest end on a note of "things are like this and it isn't right but what can we do about it?" Ultimately the answer to our protest and our questing may come first from the scientist's laboratory, just as so many of our modern questions arose there; but the stage will furnish the platform for demonstrating the answer in terms of life-situations—life foreshortened, intensified, *dramatized*. Necessarily the stage will be a little bit behind the laboratory. For that matter, it has always been a shade behind the times even when it seemed most of the moment, for ideas have to undergo a period of gestation before they take on life in any art form. So, in a sense, the plays we see upon the stage today are the scientific treatises of yesterday, and the plays of tomorrow are being written in the laboratories of today. Since the physicists are now changing their minds a bit about the nature of matter, we may get

11

some startling new effects upon tomorrow's stage, perhaps even new dimensions for tragedy. Matter, the physicists are now saying, is not the predictable entity it appeared to be such a short time ago. Instead, they say, it is an immaterial element called "force," which does not behave with strict causality. Thus they are opening the doors to new speculation, new wonder. And by wonder, says Plato, we are saved.

Not that wonder is anything new upon the stage. Of course we have always had it. It is one aspect of the grandeur which clings even to the most psychiatric of tragedies. We have always had man the pigmy in the presence of a Fate irrevocable, relentless, awe-inspiring. And man has not really changed much; it is only our greater understanding of his moods and manners that has changed a bit. Nor has our idea of Fate really changed. It is only the face of Fate that alters. That face is no longer masked by an oracle; Fate no longer comes down as a god in a machine. Today Fate is the Social Order, the Inequality of Classes, the Economic Cause of a Submerged Fraction. Or he may wear the guise of "Ole Davil Sea" or the Dust Bowl Drought. But whatever we call him, he still operates to defeat man; and as long

12

as the dramatist reflects the maladjustments about him, we will still have tragedies for the stage.

Perhaps "maladjustment" is the best word out of our current vocabulary to apply to tragedy. Tragedy is the study of a maladjustment. Of permanent maladjustment. But *when* is a character *permanently* maladjusted? When is he destined to battle unceasingly against a universal law with which he is out of focus? When, in brief, is defeat *inevitable?* On the answer to this question hinges our final response. Or perhaps we should say that the answer hinges on the implications which the playwright seems to make; and so often today's playwrights give only the implication, leaving us to make the final answer for ourselves. Maladjustment is probably permanent and defeat inevitable whenever the individual refuses to compromise with circumstances which cannot be altered without his giving up something—or some quality—which he will not give up. Thus Lear, through his pride, made himself hopelessly maladjusted; the Macbeths through their ambition made themselves hopelessly so. But Cyrano, on the other hand, makes large and gallant compromise when he must. He can never let a nose or an unrequited love unbalance him from a way of life that romps on from one calamity to another, all of which

13

he meets with the philosophy of humor until he dies at the happy ending, leaning against a tree, his plume "unblemished and unbent."

There is no categorical answer to this question, "When is maladjustment permanent?" because we all bring to our answer our own philosophy of life; we bring the assorted materials which make up our individual store of knowledge, our own experience, and our own peculiar emotional makeup. We are differently "conditioned" to find tragedy or comedy in a given situation. Obviously some situations lend themselves more readily than others to such difference of interpretation. For instance, it has never seemed possible to get anything like unanimity of opinion concerning one of the earliest of our contemporary plays, Eugene O'Neill's *Anna Christie*. If that play is a tragedy, then someone in the play goes up against the Universal to his inevitable catastrophe. At the end of the play—if it is a tragedy—we see man the pigmy going on to the sure defeat that awaits all men out of line with Things As They Have To Be. But *who* in that play battles *what* toward what end? Or is battered toward what end? Is it Anna? Is it Chris? Or is it, in its larger implications, simply Man against Fate?

The play begins when Anna comes to her father.

Chris had sent her, when she was a little child, to a farm in Minnesota, away from the sea which he feels has been the ruin in one way and another of all the rest of his family. At twenty she comes back unexpectedly. Her life, through circumstance, has been by no means the virtuous one old Chris has visioned; but when he first sees her at Jimmy-the-Priest's, he sees only what he had dreamed of seeing and not the reality which is so patent to everyone else present. He mistakes her tawdry finery and her good looks for inland gentility. He leads her happily off to his barge, and a few days later the barge pulls out for Boston. Anna responds to the sea as if she had found there something which she had missed and been looking for.

I seem to have forgot everything that's happened, and I feel clean, somehow . . . . happier than I've ever been anywhere before! It's nutty for me to feel that way.

Then one night, up from the foggy sea, comes Mat, a lusty Irish stoker who has been rescued from a shipwreck. He proceeds gaily and fervently to fall in love with the Swedish girl. He brags, he threatens, he courts her; and finally he tells old Chris that he means to marry her. Resentful, jealous, deeply anxious that Anna shall marry a man with a job on land, Chris works himself into a rage and springs at

Mat with his knife. In the midst of the fight Anna comes on deck, and in a kind of honest desperation tells the two men the true story of her life in Minnesota. Although Mat has loudly insisted that no reason she can think of for not marrying him will make the slightest difference to him, he is stunned and bewildered and angered by her disclosure. All her protests that she has never loved any man before mean nothing to him. He has been tricked. By her. By life. He'd like to kill her but he can't quite do it. Instead, he goes ashore to get "dead rotten drunk so I'll not remember if 'twas ever born you was at all." Spent with anguish and grief, Anna wearily sends Chris ashore to get drunk also.

In a couple of days her father comes back. Anna has bought a ticket for New York and is packed to go, but she cannot leave. She is waiting for Mat, even though she feels he will never return. But he does return. He can't forget her, no matter how drunk he is. He hates her but he wants her. In a way, Anna understands his hurt resentment; but she is baffled too, because the one central fact of her life is so overwhelming—she *loves* him, and she never loved a man before. What else could matter? Certainly not those bleak dreadful days in Minnesota. The sea—and Mat—have made those days as if they never were. Meanwhile, Mat's longing to believe her begins to smother out his doubt. After all, in the whole hard thirty years of his life there was never another woman he wanted to marry. From his pocket he takes an old crucifix his mother had given him, and makes Anna swear "a terrible fearful oath" that he is indeed the only man she ever loved. Then (although filled with misgiving because she isn't a Catholic and her oath may not mean all it should) his passion overrides his doubts, and he shouts a kind of challenge to Fate.

Oath or no oath, 'tis no matter. We'll be wedded in the morning, with the help of God. . . . . We'll be happy now, the two of us, in spite of the divil!

Chris comes forth for the celebration, hatred giving way to relief that Anna is so happy. But then the father learns that he and Mat are both sailing to-morrow on the same ship, each having signed on without the other's knowledge; and Chris broods again.

It's queer, yes—you and me shipping on same boat dat vay. It ain't right. . . . . It's dat funny vay ole davil sea do her vorst tricks, yes.

Anna assures the men that it is better for them to go.

We'll need the money. . . . . I'll get a little house some-where and I'll make a regular place for you two to come back to—wait and see.

17

But Chris looks out into the somber night.

Fog, fog, fog, all bloody time. You can't see vhere you vas going, no. Only dat ole davil, sea—she knows!

The two stare at him. From the harbor comes the muffled, mournful wail of steamers' whistles.

The Curtain Falls

Well—what happened *after* the curtain fell? Our answer to that question is our classification of the play.

O'Neill drops his curtain on the apparently indeterminate note. "Only dat ole davil, sea—she knows!" Fate in the guise of "ole davil sea," working defeat as inexorable as any decreed by the gods. Fate lurking in the economic order which set the pattern of Anna's experience and would keep on setting the pattern of her life, and of Mat's life and Chris's, after the men went off to sea again. Fate by means of today's psychological implications which sees Anna's personality pattern as something already set by habits of life. Even if she found the little house, would she wait for Mat through his long voyages to the ends of the earth? Or would she fail, and repent, and fail again, and wear out her life in remorse and bitterness, prolonging the inevitable defeat of character by circumstance? Or did she actually have the essential simplicity she seemed to have when she stood on deck in the fog of the harbor and felt that she was at last free of her past? Was she, perhaps, "redeemed through love" after the manner of grand tragedy, even though her words were coarse and frequently profane in the manner of contemporary tragedy's realism when dealing with ordinary people in ignoble situations? And what happened to Mat and Chris when they were once more in the clutch of "ole davil sea"—with their wages signed over to Anna? Were they giving her security or temptation? *Just what happened afterward?*

O'Neill himself was clearly unwilling to give the answer, just as apparently he was some time in determining exactly whose play it was to be, Anna's or her father's, as is indicated by the several titles he used or thought of using before he finally named the play for Anna. In its earliest version it was called *Chris Christopherson*, and it was definitely the play of the old salt when it came to a brief Atlantic City tryout with Lynn Fontanne creating the role which later, in its developed form, became so associated with the name of Pauline Lord. During the process of re-writing he called the new version, tentatively, *Dat Ole Davil*. But, still another title contemplated is the one which points directly to the uncertainty he intended to leave at the fall of the curtain.

That other title was *Comma*. "The happy ending," he observed later in explaining his intention, "is merely the comma at the end of a gaudy introductory clause, with the body of the sentence still unwritten." This assertion seems to leave no doubt of the playwright's wish that the indeterminateness of his play be recognized, but he has himself amplified the thought.

> My ending seems to have a false definiteness about it that is misleading—a happy-ever-after which I did not intend. I rely on the father's last speech of superstitious uncertainty to let my theme flow through and on. . . . . In short, all of them at the end have a vague foreboding that, although they have had their moment, the decision still rests with the sea which has achieved the conquest of Anna.

In spite of O'Neill's insistence that the play goes on uncertainly after the curtain falls, the play is tragedy *if* we feel that Anna's maladjustment is permanent. Even so, this indecisiveness is a long way removed from the old tragedy whose figures marched in a sort of majesty to the destiny of their doom. These contemporary figures move uncertainly—with dread, as Chris moved out to sea; or with defiance, as Mat decided on marriage; or with an unsure gaiety like Anna's—toward an end which neither they nor we can designate.

But whatever question may lurk in some minds as

to the authenticity of *Anna Christie* as a tragedy, no one can be in doubt that O'Neill gave us tragedy when he wrote *Desire Under the Elms*. Here certainly is the story of poor frail human pigmies torn and tortured by passions that push them to their doom with awesome certainty—a play over which broods an atmosphere of inexorable Fate from the sound of its title to the feel of its denouement, when the sheriff takes off Eben and Abbie, destroyed but exultant. There is no doubt about the finality of this play. When Abbie smothers their baby in order to prove to Eben that she really loves him (although at the beginning she had meant to trick him into fathering a child so that her husband might think it was his own and therefore make it the heir to the farm property), she is making the last convincing gesture of which she is capable. No doubt the circumstances of the story are to a portion of any audience repellent. In hate, revenge, avarice, lust, and selfishness the characters snarl and snap at one another; their language is uncouth, their purposes are low. But even so, when circumstances grind through these outer layers of ugliness, there emerges something simple, sincere, something even beautiful. To the limits of her warped nature Abbie proffered tenderness when she tried to express a feeling of motherliness for Eben in his

21

loneliness. And at the end of the play, when the sheriff comes to take her off after the infanticide, she is not sorry that she did the deed. She has proved herself to Eben. Out of all her sorry twisted life she has finally done something selfless, something triumphant. If we have to finish this story as it must have gone on after the final curtain, we assume that Eben's father is left alone gnawing away at the empty days, knowing they can give his hopes no nourishment. We assume that Abbie and Eben are convicted of murder. But even if they are not convicted, we know that they are still defeated, for they cannot in any way escape the old man or escape the memories of their guilt. Nor escape themselves.

Finality is just as certain in *All God's Chillun Got Wings* with its smashing, agonizing realization of Fate in Jim's last confidence, when Ella asks with childlike simplicity, "Will God forgive me, Jim?" and Jim answers,

> Maybe He can forgive what you've done to me; and maybe He can forgive what I've done to you; but I don't see how He's going to forgive—Himself.

After this speech we are ready for that final moment which comes so fast upon Jim's bewilderment and brings down the curtain as he "throws himself on

22

his knees and raises his shining eyes, his transfigured face."

It is easy to understand after seeing some of these O'Neill plays what he means when he speaks of "happiness" as essentially an "exaltation; an intensified feeling of the significant worth of man's being and becoming . . . . not the smirking contentment with one's lot." He has stated this credo of exaltation definitely and emphatically. "There is more of it," he asserts, "in one tragedy than in all the happy-ending plays ever written. . . . . The Greeks and the Elizabethans knew. . . . . They felt the tremendous lift of it. It roused them spiritually to deeper understanding of life. Through it they found release from the petty considerations of everyday existence." To accomplish his purpose of exaltation, O'Neill sometimes seems to train the telescope wrong-end-to in order to show us how puny man is; but in the very limitations of his field of vision and in the vividness of his presentation, he accomplishes largeness.

If one refrains from listing *Strange Interlude* and *Mourning Becomes Electra*, it is because they may be, just possibly, too especially of our own day with its preoccupation with psychoses. Not that the materials peculiar to our own day make less convincing tragedy, but that too close absorption with any materials may distort ultimate perspective. It may be, therefore, that these plays will go down as museum pieces rather than as stalwart companions of the Greeks. At least we can understand the eager inquirer who brings the O'Neill plays into a letter apropos of a recently renewed interest in *Hamlet*.

Did it ever occur to you as it did to me the other night—but of course it must have done so—that we could hardly make a tragedy today out of the story elements of *Hamlet*? Could we possibly be perturbed enough ourselves to be convinced by Hamlet's distress over the fact that the queen married his uncle? Not that we refuse to accept such abnormality as there may be, but that we tend to say "messy" and turn away in disgust as from the psychologically unnatural, rather than blame the queen as someone essentially wicked. Witness *Strange Interlude* and *Mourning Becomes Electra*. I felt withdrawal before both those plays. Not condemnation, just withdrawal. Ours is the day of institutions for those who are patently abnormal, and even paying taxes for such institutions signifies that we understand something of the psychological quirks and make allowances. Of course we are moved today when *Hamlet* is well played but our "historical sense" has to carry a heavy burden of acceptance of the story. And being able to accept the story has a big part in creating the mood of tragedy—hasn't it?

Like most inquirers, this letter-writer is "telling us" more than she is asking; but in the way she means we would be able to agree with her about *Hamlet:* we would find it hard to make a play out of the story elements today. Our public would not accept

24

all of them. Possibly she did not know that Shakespeare was writing a revenge play of the same stock model as Kyd's *The Spanish Tragedy;* and indeed we sometimes respectfully suspect that a few scholars, now and then, temporarily overlook the same fact when they strive too hard to square all inconsistencies in the Shakespeare play. For it was the something-plus which is genius that enabled Shakespeare to mold a great tragedy out of a mere revenge play. And what, after all, are a few inconsistencies when we have the greatness?

In Maxwell Anderson's revenge play of today, *Winterset,* we have subject matter as contemporary as the miscarriage of justice and people as contemporary as gangsters. And there are many who feel, with conviction for which they give reasons, that the inconsistencies so outweigh the intended loftiness of mood that *Winterset* is, in fact, a melodrama presented in the guise of a tragedy. Thus once again, as in the case of *Anna Christie,* we are confronted with the divergence of opinion which is likely to accompany the attaching of the old labels to the new plays. Those who call *Winterset* "melodrama" point to the exciting good fortune of young Mio in locating, all in one house under a bridge by the riverside, the man who can clear the name of his father, the gangster who actually committed the murder for which his father was executed, and the girl whom he loves at first sight and who returns his love as instantly— so pure and purifying a love that it burns out of Mio the hate which had driven him to seek vindication of a cruelly wronged father, so that the boy is ready to stand unafraid before the gangster's gun instead of trying to break through the ambuscade toward escape and fulfilment. These classifiers will say, although somewhat reluctantly because of the intended sincerity of the play, that the tragic element is imposed arbitrarily by the playwright and does not grow through inevitability. Therefore they will maintain that he is really writing melodrama and pushing his story for all possible social implications, after the fashion of present-day melodrama of a more serious sort.

On the other hand, many maintain that *Winterset* illustrates a tendency in some present-day tragedies, as in older tragedies, to utilize the plot of melodrama with fully drawn characters caught in the inevitable maladjustments which belong to tragedy alone. The play is less than "grand" in the old sense but still accomplishes a kind of catharsis of the emotions, they will say; it is less patently motivated by a tragic flaw in character, more weighted to the side of circumstance's control over the individual through the very fact of the individual's being an inseparable part of the society which produced him and now, in this case, leads to the complete and inevitable defeat of the individual. This is the mark of tragedy, they feel, going further than even our new social melodrama. Granting that Anderson continually skirts melodrama as he develops his story, they point out that he has given us more of finality than have his contemporaries writing the new melodrama; that even the Heywards in *Mamba's Daughters* leave open a door of escape—if not for Hagar, certainly for Lissa and through Lissa for her race, even perhaps for society as it faces tomorrow; while Anderson not only makes death inescapable for Mio and Miriamne but makes ultimate defeat the answer to that whole part of society they represent—or at least suggests that any open door of escape for society is down such a far vista as to seem more illusion than reality.

Part of the feeling of tragedy which Anderson has imparted to *Winterset* comes from his use of the poetic form for his dialogue. Many persons, erroneously or not, are more easily persuaded that a play is a tragedy when it comes to their ears in measured phrasings. During these first decades of the century we have proceeded in the theater from realism of

27

setting through realism of acting to a keener realism of thinking on the part of the playwright, and now seem to be at the point of keeping the realistic thinking while trying to get nearer the true illusion of drama by discarding some of the exterior trappings of realism; and Anderson tries the experiment, using not only the poetic medium but a contemporary theme and contemporary people. His story, as we have indicated, is the melodramatic story of young Mio and his determination to clear his father's name until love wipes out his hate.

Mio is a boy in his late teens when he comes back from the aimless hitchhiking existence he has led since the conviction and execution of his father at the hands of the state. He has chanced upon a clue which makes him think that someone has evidence of his father's innocence, evidence which might now convict the real murderer. His sleuthings lead him to a dilapidated tenement on the waterfront. On a dark rainy night he meets Miriamne, a frail sensitive girl of the tenement, and falls in love with her. He also meets Garth, a young violin-player whose testimony might have saved Mio's father if Garth had not been afraid of Trock Estrella, the real murderer, and his gang. Mio does not know that Garth is Miriamne's brother. While Mio is in Garth's tenement home trying to find out if Garth has any new evidence which he could present at a new trial, old Judge Gaunt wanders into the place. He is dignified, well dressed; but his mind is clouded from much self-incrimination over his own part as trial judge in the widely discussed Romagna case. This night he is sane enough to present so moving an account of his side of the famous case that Mio's faith in his father's innocence is shaken. But Trock also happens in, is startled to discover who Mio is, and fears a ruse. From all their defenses and threats Mio pieces together the true story, realizes that Trock is the murderer, and tries to hand him over to an officer who comes to take the meandering old judge home. But the officer thinks Mio is merely "kidding him out of his uniform pants," as he has done once before in a street fracas, and pays no attention. Mio finds that the girl he loves is the sister of the man whose testimony might have saved his father; now he cannot take his revenge if he would. And he no longer wants it. Miriamne persuades him that his father would have forgiven, that he would not want justice which will cost more lives, more heartbreak. Released from the need to avenge his father's death, Mio promises to try to escape Trock's inevitable attempt to put him out of the way, and to keep in touch with Miriamne; but he is shot down by Trock's henchmen. Then Miramne, crying out her knowledge of the murderers, is killed beside him.

Out of these incidents Anderson might easily have made unmistakable melodrama. Only a slight further shifting of emphasis from character to situation, a quick turn to a conventionally happy ending (as was done in the screen version), a bit more emphasis on sentimental moralities, and the play would have given no chance whatsoever for diverging opinions. It would have stepped out of the tragedy category, undeniably. However, since Anderson presumably did not intend to do any of these things but instead intended to show characters swept along to inevitable death by forces beyond their control, it may seem fair enough to look at his play as he himself must look at it—which would be to call it a "variety of contemporary tragedy" if we were reaching for a label. Thus looked at, the characters of *Winterset* may seem so motivated as to take on a larger significance, to have about them some of the element of grandeur which was a requisite of the older tragedy, common and contemporary as these characters are—as common and contemporary, in fact, as the hitchhikers we are forever seeing thumbing their way so definitely toward the most indefinite of destinations. Mio—young, economically helpless, bewildered—is driven by so strong a purpose that at least in the earlier scenes of the play he seems to reach a stature beyond the average man's. Miriamne too, young as she is, is not confused by appearances but feels her way to the truth of things with the intuition of a child. We sense the quality with which Anderson wishes to endow these two when Mio first sends Miriamne back into the house, where his love cannot touch her.

Mio: And tell them when you get inside where it's warm, and you love each other, and mother comes to kiss her darling, tell them to hang onto it while they can, believe while they can it's a safe warm world, and Jesus finds his lambs and carries them in his bosom. I've seen some lambs that Jesus missed. If they ever want the truth, tell them that nothing's guaranteed in this climate except it gets cold in winter, nor on this earth except you die sometime.

Miriamne: I have no mother. And my people are Jews.

Mio: Then you do know something about it.

Miriamne: Yes.

Mio: Do you have enough to eat?

Miriamne: Not always.

Mio: What do you believe in?

Miriamne: Nothing.

Mio: Why?

Miriamne: How can one?

Mio: It's easy if you're a fool. You see the words in books. Honor, it says there, chivalry, freedom, heroism, enduring

31

love—and these are words on paper. It's something to have them there. You'll get them nowhere else.

MIRIAMNE: What hurts you?

MIO: Just that. You'll get them nowhere else.

MIRIAMNE: Why should you want them?

MIO: I'm alone, that's why. . . . .

As the play proceeds, the playwright plainly wishes us to feel that Miriamne gives so much of love which has understanding at its heart that Mio can at last transcend his own uncertainties. He can answer her with assurance deeper than any which might have come from a guaranty that Trock would make no further design upon his life.

MIO: Whatever streets I walk, you'll walk them, too,
from now on, and whatever roof or stars
I have to house me, you shall share my roof
and stars and morning. I shall not forget.

MIRIAMNE: God keep you!

MIO: And keep you. And this to remember!
If I should die, Miriamne, this half-hour
is our eternity. I came here seeking
light in darkness, running from the dawn,
and stumbled on a morning.

"Stumbled on a morning"—the impulse of meaning which the playwright wishes us to see rising from character to point the triumph behind apparent defeat.

In so contemporary a tragedy Fate, as we would

32

expect, lurks in the socioeconomic order. Forces beyond Mio's control or understanding have produced the "criminal" who committed the murder for which his father was convicted; those same forces wrought the miscarriage of justice and then sanctioned the injustice by decree of the sovereign state. Unrelenting, the same forces work on, not with the placable anger of the gods but with the impersonality of some vast, diabolical machine. And yet, for all the impersonality of this modern "social" Fate, it is man himself—today as with the Greeks—who rises through suffering beyond the reach of any disaster devised by Fate.

All of this, of course, *if* we can feel that *Winterset* is a tragedy, as many persons do. The feeling of. tragedy was undoubtedly further induced in the theater by the Mio of Burgess Meredith, the Miriamne of Margo, and the haunting figure of Judge Gaunt as realized by Richard Bennett.

Winterset closes on the note of love, as the same note, differently tuned, brings about the resolution in other plays by Anderson—*Night over Taos, Valley Forge, The Masque of Kings*, for instance. Some who would ask for more searching social significance in Anderson's work find fault with such a conclusion, feeling it is sentimental at worst and defeatist at best.

Others feel that Anderson reaches a human truth, if not a social one, in the final fleeting moment which he grants to Mio and Miriamne.

No such moment is meted out to the awkward, inarticulate man who is the tragic central figure of *Ethan Frome.* (Of course we knew the tragedy of Ethan's life before it reached the stage, but Owen and Donald Davis—plus the stagecraft elements of production and the interpretations of Raymond Massey, Pauline Lord, and Ruth Gordon—have so fully transferred Mrs. Wharton's novel to the stage that it lives again in this other medium.) Ethan's tragedy knows no final moment of release. *His* tragedy lies in necessary adjustment to a continuing, torturing maladjustment. It seems to be "pure" tragedy because Ethan, like Prometheus, is chained to circumstances which make it inevitable that the vultures shall tear at him anew each day. One hunts for the tragic flaw in him. Was it weakness which made him marry the capable woman seven years his senior who had taken care of his "queer" old mother during her long last illness? Or was it a kind of cosmic loneliness as stark as the rocky New England farm from which he tried to wrest a living? And if the latter, may such loneliness be itself a weakness, and therefore akin to a tragic flaw? At least, when his wife turns into a whining, ailing, self-centured hypochondriac, we do not feel that it is weakness in Ethan which makes him give way to her. She is now just one more of his responsibilities, like the starved little farm and the decrepit mill. Throughout the play, Frome is a creature of circumstance.

Perhaps in this we see again today's modification of tragedy. There is nothing in Ethan which can compromise; he is made as he is by forces over which he never had any control. When he falls in love with his wife's gay young "poor relation" who has come to do the work of a "hired girl," his is the inarticulate love of a stalwart taciturn man who cannot make his devotion into the kind of scheming craftiness which might have freed them. Poverty—just plain lack of enough money to buy railway tickets—prevents his escape with the girl. The decision of Zeena, grown vindictively suspicious, to send Mattie away is as final a decree as anything the Grecian gods might have wrought. Behind the wife, if she chooses to lean on it, stands public opinion. The girl cannot stay, Ethan cannot go; their love is the one enduring tenderness either has ever known, and life would be drab past all bearing without it— or so they seem to know that it would be. Until after the final wild ride down the icy hill. Was that last wild ride together the impulse of a tragic flaw? Yet the plunge down the hill seems less defiance of Fate than a sudden rising to full-size stature; like a desperate joyous reaching for a spiritual fulfilment in the moment—not too unlike the "eternity in a moment" which was granted to young Mio and the younger Miriamne. But for Ethan Frome and Mattie there is no gangster lurking in the shadows to send the swift release of death. These two are not allowed to measure their highest height against eternity. None of the full realization that came to Mio and Miriamne so briefly, and none of the grand climactic finish of the old tragedy, is theirs. Instead, they are maimed for life, both of them; taken back to the ugly house on the barren farm, the girl never to walk again and Ethan to go on with his daily work in spite of a twisted, awkward body. Even so, there might have been a triumphant comprehension between the two which would deepen with the years. But pain and inaction wear the buoyant, sensitive girl into another whining old woman, quarreling with Ethan's wife, day in, day out. If Ethan, too, had degenerated into a quarreling old man. . . . . But he didn't; he maintained his stature. . . . . Perhaps here is the thin spire of meaning which, accord-

ing to our earlier teaching, rises from all true tragedy. In an older tradition Oedipus could blind his
own eyes and go out into the world—somewhere,
we don't know where—but Ethan has to stay on,
maimed in body and desolate in spirit, struggling
for a useless survival in the economic setup, watching
the maladjustments around him and made constantly aware of his own maladjustment; merely
closing in silently upon himself.

Life goes on after the final curtain falls. If there
can be a question about the later days of Anna
Christie and of Chris and Mat, there can be none
about these trapped characters of Mrs. Wharton's
story. When we come to the final page of her novel
—when the Davises drop their curtain on the dramatization—we *know*. All doors are closed. For Ethan,
for Mattie, for Zeena. And the release of death for
the one—any one of them—would bring no help to
the others, would take away no torture. Nothing in
circumstance or in himself can possibly free Ethan
Frome. This is a sort of ending which we are likely
to find in tragedies today; not always of course, but
frequently. The ending which denies a character
the fatal finality of most of the older tragedies; the
newer finality which closes all doors and then com-
pels the defeated to live on. If Ethan Frome had

had a god to defy, or a tragic flaw in the sense of
some moral shortcoming which he might strive to
overcome, his tragedy might be less devastating, or
even more exalting. But it would be less in the contemporary mood.

Mrs. Wharton writes tragedy in terms of the
bleak environment of a New England farm and a
frustrated New England farmer; Anderson in terms
of gangsters and tenements, of class feeling and the
miscarriage of justice. Robert Turney, with a feeling
equally contemporary, writes in terms of an ancient
story. Not a classical story jazzed up to farce tempo
to make us laugh at the predicaments of our day
in the looking-glass of the ancients; not an old story
slanted for satire or political commentary; but
straight tragedy in terms of heroic characters who
presume to take personal exception to the decrees
of the gods and are defeated through final and overwhelming catastrophe. Gathering together into one
the several stories of the house of Atreus—of Agamemnon, Iphegeneia, Elektra—he nevertheless gives
us a play which seems as up-to-now as an air raid
or compulsory conscription, as present-day as a psychoanalytic laboratory, as contemporary as the
skilled lighting which helps to set the play's mood—
the simulation of sunlight, the tracery of leaves, far

blue skies, depth of shadow, the open sea, the threat of storm—and as contemporary, also, as the careful use of color at once lavish and restrained which makes both setting and costumes an integral part of the drama in a manner distinctly of today even while their effect is the heightening of that emotional awareness which the Greeks felt was the aim of tragedy.

The face of Fate looms over *Daughters of Atreus* throughout, but it is a face of two masks: one toward the Greeks to speak through oracles, obedient winds, ancient family wrongs; the other mask turned toward the modern day to shout across the centuries the havoc wrought by twentieth-century warfare.

Klytaimnestra, the queen, rules while Agamemnon is off at the Trojan wars. In all her dealings she is mindful of the fact that their house is marked for bitter struggle one day.

There's no atonement for the crime of Agamemnon's father, Atreus. In vengeance for his ravished wife, he slew his brother's children on the holy day of Artemis, upon which day all living things are sacred to the gods. Aegisthos only was not slain and fled to Crete. This is the feud betwixt Aegisthos and my lord. Such have no end but death.

However, she is busy with affairs of state and also has a careful, tender eye for her family—the young princess Iphegeneia, who is the mother's favorite;

39

the little sister Elektra, who is not strong and keeps close to their beloved nurse, Polymnia, manager of the household; the baby son, Orestes. Then into the pleasant household a messenger comes suddenly from Agamemnon: Iphegeneia is to hasten to Aulis, where the Grecian ships await. There she shall marry the handsome young warrior, Achilles. Iphegeneia, Klytaimnestra, Polymnia—indeed, the whole court—are full of joy; and against Agamemnon's warning, Klytaimnestra joyfully accompanies Iphegeneia to Aulis.

Before the temple at Aulis, Agamemnon and Achilles await the girl with deep anxiety, for they know that she is not coming to her bridal but to her death; that the oracle has decreed that only a blood sacrifice of someone "unstained and pure" from the house of Agamemnon can bring the favorable winds for which the fleet has waited many months. The gods are angry; atonement has never yet been made for the sacrilege of Atreus. Agamemnon argues with the priest Kalchas that some other sacrifice must be found; he will not bring his wife this sorrow, "a wife so fashioned all of tenderness and dignity and warmth." Upon this scene Klytaimnestra arrives with the girl. The fatal decree is made known by Kalchas because Agamemnon cannot bring himself to say the words. The mother is momentarily stunned, then begs frantically for someone to save her daughter. Achilles springs to her side, offering to defy whatever powers have brought this thing about. Let the wars wait; there have been too many wars already. But the priest insists this is a holy war, and Agamemnon acquiesces that they are bound to Menelaos by their oath. Argument gives way to drawn sword, whereupon Iphegeneia cries for peace and silence. She is ready for the sacrifice, she says; she cannot be saved, and she would like to go quickly and with dignity.

I, who might have gone immemorably to death, am wound immortally with garlands now. I who die childless, gather all my people to my heart to be my children now. My death shall give them strength to live.

But for all the assurance of her words, she is only a girl sick with fear. It is to herself she speaks as she mounts the steps of the temple. "I am a King's daughter. I have the strength to walk alone." Upon the top she pauses a moment. "How full," she says, "—how full of sunlight the heavens are." And she moves out of sight toward the sacrificial altar. Unseen, the people chant below. The priest "remains standing against the sky, his arms lifted in prayer. His mantle hangs motionless about him in the

41

breathless air." Klytaimnestra shrieks her horror; Agamemnon is overcome with grief; the crowd is still. Then Kalchas, still standing motionless, "stretches higher his arms as though he would pluck the wind from the very sky. . . . . Suddenly his garments lift and winnow gently about him in the rising wind." The Troyward wind rouses the trumpets and voices order the sails unfurled. Agamemnon, elated even in his grief, feels that the curse is lifted from his house. He begs his wife for some token of farewell. Klytaimnestra remains motionless, unseeing. Her answer comes slowly and with terrible, quiet intensity: *"I will await your coming."* Above her stands Kalchas, "his arms still uplifted. As the wind strengthens into a gale, his blood-red mantle streams out and up against the sky until it is like some terrible wave curling above Klytaimnestra's head."

For ten years Klytaimnestra awaits her husband's coming. She sells out to his enemy, invites Aegisthos to her court, makes him her lover. Together they plan to kill Agamemnon upon his return from Troy. Elektra is a young girl now, and Orestes a sizable boy. At last one day the sails of the returning fleet are sighted, and the children are delirious with joy. Suddenly, with the moment of Agamemnon's ar-

42

rival almost upon them, Aegisthos refuses to commit the murder. He loves Klytaimnestra enough to die with her or for her; but he is no warrior, and he will not do the deed. Then Klytaimnestra, remembering the slaughter of her first-born, in a fury of revenge and bitterness seizes the ax she has made ready for the deed. . . . . "In a voice like the pounding of a heart" she repeats like a chant the name of Iphegeneia. She is ready. Her face is masklike. A moment later, however, to the joyfully returning Agamemnon her face is suddenly all smiles and seeming tenderness as she leads him into an adjoining room, according to her carefully schemed plan. She sends the children and Polymnia from her; she makes her way toward the room whither she has led her husband. A silence; then Elektra, returning, hears her father's cries for help and her mother's voice shrieking again the single word "Iphegeneia"; hears the crash of metal on shattered bone; sees her mother come from the inner room with bloodstained hands. For a moment Klytaimnestra mistakes Elektra for Iphegeneia somehow miraculously restored to her; then recognizing Elektra, swoons and is carried from the room. Elektra, torn with grief, her hair and dress disheveled, lifts a face "touched with a dedicated light of ecstasy and suffering." She calls aloud

43

to her dead father; and a low muttering of thunder answers as the curtains close on the second act.

The years go by and Klytaimnestra rules with her husband Aegisthos. The child Orestes has grown to young manhood in exile. Elektra, steeped in bitterness, lives only for the day when her brother shall return to avenge his father's death. Polymnia, grown old, is ill; and all the women of the court, including the queen, are lovingly anxious about her. The day has come for crowning of the Queen of Spring; the city prepares to celebrate. Two strange young travelers come to the court and seek out Elektra. One of them discloses himself as Orestes, whereupon Elektra, in a delirium of relief, sweeps him into her scheme for vengeance. Though Orestes is reluctant, she unfolds her plan: Tonight, while the city is in revelry, Orestes must go before the king, who will pour the cup of welcome for a stranger. He must seize that moment to strike Aegisthos down; then, returning to the queen's quarters, complete their vengeance by slaying their mother. Still reluctant, Orestes finally swears his promise.

In the evening Klytaimnestra, alone with her old nurse, cries to her,

Polymnia! . . . . I cannot bear this emptiness! Oh, teach me to be like you. What are your gods? Tell me their names and I will worship them.

But Polymnia says that her gods are nameless, one knows them only in the heart; and tries to still Klytaimnestra's nameless dread and give her peace. Presently the nurse is put back to bed, and the queen is alone. Lights move in the orchard. Then Elektra, "completely covered in a cloak of dull red copper, ... on her head a gold crown of spikes," comes to protest to the astonished queen that she means to be a daughter after all these years. Klytaimnestra, hungry for love and long estranged from the girl, is quick to welcome her. But Elektra's talk grows strange, threatening—saying nothing, saying everything; wheedling the queen into staying with her, calling her "Mother" at last. Now suddenly young Orestes appears, his identity made known to his mother by Elektra. Klytaimnestra makes an eager movement toward him . . . . then sees his bloody sword. "It is Aegisthos' blood," Elektra cries exultantly. "See, she has tears for her paramour who had no tears for Agamemnon's sake." But Klytaimnestra is not weeping for the dead king or pleading for herself—she is trying to save her children from the deed they are about to commit.

O God! Give me some power of words to sweep like flame across their minds and burn away this darkness and this hate. I will save you from yourselves.

45

Orestes would listen to her, would grant exile to her. But not Elektra; the girl recalls each detail of her father's murder. Whereupon Klytaimneśtra, unable to reason with her, tries to escape by cunning. She suddenly turns toward the shadows and speaks as if to attendants, bidding them seize the son and daughter. As Orestes turns, sword raised, to meet the ruse, the queen rushes toward the doors but cannot open them.

Her pursuers are almost upon her when with one last terrible gesture of despair she hurls the doors open and the awful hunt disappears into a flood of clean, pure moonlight and delicate tree shadows.

The women of the court come into the room to lay out the queen's robe for the night. When they go, they leave the great doors open. "The night wind will sweeten the chamber."

Then slowly onto this strangely quiet scene Orestes and Elektra return, cowering away from each other, two trembling, broken figures. "Now she can never love me," says Elektra. And Orestes answers, "She died like a queen." Elektra speaks on with growing terror in her voice; Orestes answers dully. "We must not think, Orestes," cries the girl. "Her hair was white," her brother answers. In a sudden burst of resentment against his sister, he lifts his sword . . . . then lets it drop clattering to his side. Half-mad,

46

he seems to see his mother rise before him and calls out to her. And Elektra, "exhausted and like an old, old woman, ... puts her arms around him . . . . as though he were a sick child." The door of Polymnia's room opens; and one of the maidens, still crowned with flowers, "moves quietly out into the white moonlight." She does not see Elektra and Orestes crouched in the deep shadows. "You were mistaken," she calls back to Polymnia,

> There is no one here . . . . The Queen? . . . . I think she has gone out into her garden. (*Her voice becomes ecstatic, thrilling.*) O Polymnia! . . . . The heavens are like soft transparent fire behind the stars. . . . . Yes, I hear them singing across the fields, far away and faint, but very sweet. . . . . They are moving through the night now, under the great branches; up into the holy hills. (*Her face is lifted. She stands a moment, motionless and beautiful.*) How full of light the heavens are!

Partly it is this tying-in of the forces of nature with the forces which make or break human character that gives tragedy its depth dimension. Usually the more somber aspects of nature are the ones underscored. In *King Lear* the wild storm on the heath reflects, intensifies, the old man's suffering; in *Winterset* the persistent rain that falls on Mio and Miriamne is one with the relentless social order; in *Anna Christie* the heavy fog blowing up off the sea is part of the bewilderment which smothers the three human beings. In *Daughters of Atreus*, while use is made of gathering storm and threat of thunder, the play seems to derive its peculiar atmospheric lift through the use of nature's more delicate aspects. It is a rather poignant moment when Melissa voices her young resentment against the ecstasy of spring while the grand old woman Polymnia is about to die; the extremes of human experience seem brought together in this moment. And it is made to seem right that this story should end with the exclamation, "How full of light the heavens are!"—as if behind the inscrutable universe there is some hope toward which all the participants in the play—including the audience—are swept.

The play may be cast to ancient mold, but the playwright's workmanship has something distinctly of this day in the way he so carefully lets us see the child Elektra's feeling of inferiority and need for compensation, even for overcompensation. There is her resentment against the fact that Iphegeneia is the mother's favorite—Iphegeneia, able to run in the sunshine while Elektra is made ill by strenuous play. There is her unconscious reaction toward Orestes, the brother whose birth brought such joy to the king and queen. Although she loves the baby, there is no doubt some feeling within Elektra that she is the "odd" one among the children. Later, Iphegeneia's cruel death is assuredly a blow to Elektra, but here again it raises the older sister above her; Iphegeneia has achieved a sort of radiant immortality which quite obscures Elektra's simple place in the household. When her mother brings Aegisthos to the court and with such obviousness takes him into her affections, Elektra is once more left out and begins to identify herself with the absent father. Then when the mother finally murders the father, almost before the child's eyes, the identity becomes complete: it will be herself she vindicates in avenging her father. The physical strength which has been denied her is compensated for by her unflinching strength of purpose. Her father's prowess in battle seeps into her heart to make her one with him. The very warping of her nature increases her singleness of purpose against the day when she must move Orestes to lift the ax against their mother. Although none of the vocabulary of modern psychoanalysis is there, the playwright—with conscious purpose or else in unconscious absorption of the contemporary technique —has given us a personality study very much of today.

Probably the play's greatest claim to contemporaneity, however, is in its commentary on one of the major social problems of our day—war. The sacrifice of Iphegeneia, the long drawn years of the Trojan battles, and the slow disintegration of a land and a people without the nation's manhood are the background from which Achilles' anger rises.

O gray-beards! You of old have made your wars for this or that; stirring with the threat of fire divine or moving with an equal empty hope of glory restless youths to hate and lust of blood; while women sit in grief at home, and there behind the burning veil of stars the very soul of God cries out in pain of it. This earth is wide and fair and rich. There is enough for every man that tills and sows and reaps and garners what he reaps. What is this lust for the storied towers of gold, for ocean-polished stones and earth-embedded gems? For this it is that draws you on and not your wounded honor, as you claim. Is there a quarrel, be it howsoever great, that justifies the countless dead who, living, might have ministered to men? . . . .

. . . . No war is holy! I whom you know am unafraid to fight repeat no war is holy and no war is just.

When the people, stirred by their leaders, clamor for war and grow restless because the fleet is delayed at Aulis, then religion comes forth in guise of the high priest not only to bless the undertaking but to bolster up its own prestige and save its pride by demanding atonement for the sins of Iphegeneia's grandfather. The priest in the flaming robe, sanctifying slaughter, stands in sharp contrast to the deeply religious feeling for life which is Polymnia's—

50

Polymnia, whose gods dwell "only in the heart"; who can recount the gentle life of her young days when she herself was a queen with a king who loved her and with an infant son of her own; who lived in splendor until Agamemnon's father sacked her city, killed her husband and child, and brought her back to Greece to be nurse to the baby Klytaimnestra; who can now speak serenely of the peace which replaced bitterness in her heart since she has learned to meet each day as it comes with a full measure of work and patience. The high priest spoke for the temporal power of religion, Polymnia for the spirit; both spoke to their own day, and both speak to ours. Of course the social consequences inherent in the struggle between religion-of-authority and religion-of-the-spirit is probably as old as the race. But the playwright seems to be speaking a special word to the present day when church and state are welding new bonds and shouting new defiance in so many parts of the world and when integrity of character seems at a premium.

Thus *Daughters of Atreus*, retelling the story of ancient Greeks as maladjusted in a world of gods and oracles and ordained vengeances, becomes the tragedy of today, with these ancient characters moved by the push and pull of psychological forces

51

which the contemporary audience can readily understand; and with such social forces as led to the Trojan
War giving interpretation or protest to some of the
forces which baffle our own generation, until we
accept the Turney play from and with the viewpoint
of today as easily as we understand and accept the
motivations, frustrations, implications of plays like
Anna Christie and *Desire Under the Elms, Winterset* and
Ethan Frome.

Analyze them as we may, for whatever reason and
from whatever angle, the basic qualities of tragedy
remain the same: unresolvable maladjustment
whether it ends in the finality of death or a futile
lingering on, the defeat of the individual by some
great eternal force beyond his control, grandeur of
mood, and in the end that lifting of the human emotions which the Greeks called "catharsis." If the
play is of our day, it cannot escape the vocabulary of
our day—the vocabulary of ideas and attitudes and
philosophic suppositions as well as of words. But
the tragedy of today, if it is really great tragedy, is
no more restricted by its timeliness than the older
tragedies which have come down to us. For human
character—with its essential tragedy—goes on much
the same.

II.

COMEDIES WITHOUT A LAUGH

AS A RULE, WHEN WE ARE TOLD THAT WE ARE GOING to see a comedy we expect to be entertained by ludicrous situations. We expect to laugh. For most of us have a tendency when we *hear* the word "comedy" to *think* the word "farce." And indeed in this prompt reaction to the word we are historically correct, since comedy was originally farce when in ancient days it romped into drama as a sort of poor relation. In the days of the Greeks comedy at first consisted largely in antics and buffoonery to which jibes and jests were gradually added. But sometimes the jester was a "character" who reminded one vaguely of Uncle Philo, let us say, or of the little old man with the squint eye who sold daggers in the shop on the Street of the Conquerors. His antics were still funny, but one could not always laugh aloud because Uncle Philo was a lonesome devil in spite of his buffoonery in the market place, and the old man who sold daggers was a hero if you knew his family life. And so,

53

with characterization steadily developing as time
went on, and with motivation leading to consequence and thus developing into story, comedy became something more than farce. If it was less hilariously funny, it was sometimes more amusing. Or
was it "amusing," really, when one thought it over?
The long view may check a laugh mid-air. At any
rate, as man became more aware of himself, more
self-conscious about the society of which he was a
part, he tended to shift some of his problems out of
the somber framework of tragedy into the everyday
setting of comedy which dealt with people like himself, not always heroic and not always defeated. So
the playwright through the centuries dealt more and
more with comedy, evolving his increasingly lifelike
situations out of the inconsistencies, the incongruities, the indiosyncracies of human nature.

This material of comedy changes very little from
one generation to another (human nature being
such a hardy perennial), though today our playwrights may arrange their materials in patterns
which seem to us quite different from any the world
has dealt with before, on the stage or off. Yet now,
as always, the material of comedy is character, just
as the material of tragedy is character. Characters
in a situation. What the characters do with the situa-

tion—or what the situation does with the characters
—depends upon the kind of characters they are. In
tragedy, as we have seen, characters struggle with
the inevitable to their certain defeat; but in comedy
they struggle toward their possible release, their adjustment, their "happiness." In a light comedy they
struggle blithely, either very much in earnest about
unimportant ends or very casual over important
ends; at least they never plow deep enough to turn
up the roots of sinister motivation or to expose hid-
den caches of philosophic thought. In comedy of
manners the characters struggle smartly, catching
their heels on the uncertain steps of "sophistication"
and sometimes going down on their aristocratic
noses but never to the genuine catastrophe of their
physiognomy or the permanent disarrangement of
their own—or society's—polite attire. In heroic comedy the characters struggle grandly, with lordly gesture and frequently with lordly speech, making noble
sacrifices which never seem too sad because the sacrifice is likely to be decked with the spirit of waving
plumes and acclaimed by a shouting populace. In
still other comedies, neither light nor sophisticated
nor romantic, the characters seem to struggle more
or less nondescriptly in about the fashion we ourselves struggle day in and day out, contending with

55

circumstances as they arise and expecting to escape any ultimate knockout. Much of the struggle around us in life seems to be of this sort—just naturally incongruous enough so that we know it is the struggle of comedy. There is our neighbor who works eight hours a day at an adding-machine in order to buy gas enough to spend eight hours a night in a car; there is our aunt who spends her money at auctions buying antique beds when she can't sleep nights anyway; there is our cousin who lives next door to a schoolyard and has had his study soundproofed so that he can write a book on the psychology of boys at play; and here we are ourselves rushing around getting ready to go some place where we don't want to be—struggle aplenty, but comedy. We admit it. Indeed, in certain moods we publicize it. "Comedy," we say; "you and I and life rushing for a train we don't need to catch or wool-gathering while the only bus to our Destination passes us by." In these moods we can look at ourselves—even at ourselves—in the spirit of comedy. And it is easy enough to catch the same keynote of comedy when it is put upon the stage.

We all have the quick response of comedy when, in Clifford Goldsmith's *What a Life*, young Henry

Aldrich, "his hair neither combed nor uncombed," is uneasily present in that least alluring section of a city high school, the principal's office; hears the principal put that least welcome of inquiries, "What is your home address?" and then sees him scratching off the fateful letter to Henry's parents. We understand both Henry *and* the principal as Mr. Bradley "licks the envelope with relish" and remarks,

> I wonder whether your mother won't be a trifle upset when you hand her this?
>
> HENRY: My father will be even more upset.
>
> MR. BRADLEY: Could you do anything else if you were in my position?
>
> HENRY: I think I'd give myself another chance, Mr. Bradley. You don't understand my parents. Sometimes, even I don't understand them.

Comedy of course—familiar characters in a not unfamiliar situation; at some time we too have been on a spot in a principal's office, or we have known kids who have been.

The response of comedy is just as quickly sure when we first come upon the Miller family getting ready for the Fourth of July fireworks in Eugene O'Neill's *Ah, Wilderness!* And we smile with sympathetic amusement when later on young Richard Miller sits in the moonlight on the beach waiting

57

for Muriel to come, and soliloquizes—as we ourselves once talked to ourselves while waiting for a girl (or a boy).

RICHARD *is discovered sitting sideways on the gunwale of the rowboat near the stern. He is facing left, watching the path. He is in a great state of anxious expectancy, squirming about uncomfortably on the narrow gunwale, kicking at the sand restlessly, twirling his straw hat, with a bright-colored band in stripes, around on his finger.*

RICHARD (*thinking aloud*): Must be nearly nine. . . . . I can hear the Town Hall clock strike, it's so still tonight. . . . . Gee, I'll bet Ma had a fit when she found out I'd sneaked out. . . . . I'll catch hell when I get back, but it'll be worth it . . . . if only Muriel turns up . . . . she didn't say for certain she could . . . . gosh, I wish she'd come! . . . . am I sure she wrote nine? . . . . (*He puts the straw hat on the seat amidships and pulls the folded letter out of his pocket and peers at it in the moonlight.*) Yes, it's nine, all right.

Now we see Richard "jump to his feet restlessly"; hear him "try to think of something else . . . . that'll make the time pass quicker," voicing thoughts not different from adolescent thoughts in any period though Richard is waiting for *his* girl back in 1906; hear him sigh as he "stares around him at the night."

Gee, it's beautiful tonight . . . . as if it was a special night . . . . for me and Muriel. . . . . Gee, I love tonight. . . . . I love the sand, and the trees, and the grass, and the water and the sky, and the moon . . . . it's all in me and I'm in it. . . . . God, it's so beautiful! (*He stands staring at the moon with a rapt face. From the distance the Town Hall clock begins to strike. This brings him back to earth with a start.*) There's nine now. . . . . (*He peers at the path apprehensively.*) I don't see her . . . . she must have got caught. . . . . (*Almost tearfully.*) Gee, I hate to go home and catch hell . . . . without having seen her! . . . . (*Then calling a manly cynicism to his aid.*) Aw, who ever heard of a woman ever being on time. . . . . I ought to know enough about life by this time not to expect. . . . . (*Then with sudden excitement.*) There she comes now. . . . . Gosh! (*He heaves a huge sigh of relief—then recites dramatically to himself, his eyes on the approaching figure.*)

"And lo my love, mine own soul's heart, more dear
Than mine own soul, more beautiful than God,
Who hath my being between the hands of her—"

(*Then hastily.*) Mustn't let her know I'm so tickled. . . . . I ought to be about that first letter, anyway . . . . if women are too sure of you, they treat you like slaves . . . . let her suffer, for a change. . . . . (*He starts to stroll around with exaggerated carelessness, turning his back on the path, hands in pockets, whistling with insouciance "Waiting at the Church."*)

Comedy is apparent enough when we can look back with the literal perspective of years at youth which took itself so seriously, which felt itself so uniquely. Trouble in school, trouble in love—we know now that poignant as they are while they are happening those things have no relation to real trouble. It is funny *now* that we were so serious *then*. Yet it does not help much to wonder if the things we think so serious now will be funny at some future time. For comedy is seldom funny when we are

59

going through the experience. That's why it is comedy when it happens to the other fellow: because someone else lacks our perspective to distinguish the incidental from the truly pertinent. Looking fore or aft, life is comedy when other people get their ambitions and actions and emotions and reactions out of focus with our own light. Perhaps it seems especially "comedy" that we—who now have so much light— were ever alarmed by the shadows of reality which frightened Henry and Richard.

It is not only youth that we can see from the perspective of our own experiences. Older persons also can be out of focus—any person, in fact, whose experience gives him a set of values different from our own. When other people work hard for something we don't want, we say, "Aren't they funny!" When they are bowled over by circumstances which wouldn't fease us, or preen themselves on praise we wouldn't care for, or give up their leisure and their ease for ends we don't consider gains, we say again, "Aren't they funny!" We mean, of course, "They're different from us." And yet we know how "different" they are only because we know how like us they really are. That's comedy—and it is sometimes pretty serious.

We know it is comedy which we are seeing when

the curtain first goes up on Irwin Shaw's *The Gentle People* and we behold two old men in a boat fishing by night in the East River and hear them wishing, planning, scheming, for a chance to buy a thirty-five-foot boat that will take them off to warmer waters for bigger fish. They are "funny that way."

JONAH: Off the coast of Cuba, in the Gulf Stream, they catch fish that weigh between 700 and 1000 pounds. Fish with spears on their noses. The water's warm and the sun shines eleven months a year.

PHILIP: It sounds like music, like music from a band.

JONAH: You and me, we could be sitting in the middle of the Gulf Stream, with panama hats, fishing for fish with spears in their noses. You and me.

PHILIP: That is definitely too good to be true. Definitely.

JONAH: Sometimes, Philip, you make me sick.

PHILIP: If there is something good in the air, it doesn't happen to me.

JONAH: Swanson says he will sell the boat for five hundred dollars. It is a thirty-five-foot boat. It has two bunks and a kitchen.

PHILIP: A galley. On a boat it's called a galley.

JONAH: Two bunks and a galley. All right. In a thirty-five-foot boat with two bunks and a galley it is possible in mild weather to go down the coast to Florida. Right or wrong?

PHILIP: I'm not arguing with you.

JONAH (*steadfastly continuing*): If we buy the boat from Swanson, what is to prevent us from finally sitting in the middle of the Gulf Stream with panama hats? (*Triumphantly.*) Nothing!

61

ABC, it's proved. (*He gets a bite and starts reeling in.* ANAGNOS *sighs.*)

PHILIP: It isn't so bad here. There are worse places to be on a winter night than Steeplechase Pier.

JONAH (*contemptuously*): A Greek! A fine Greek! In the old days the Greeks used to travel a thousand miles in a rowboat.

PHILIP: That was a different kind of Greek from me, Jonah. (JONAH *pulls in the fish.*) Is it good?

JONAH: Pah! (*He unhooks the fish and throws it back.*) Go home to your mamma. Come back in two years.

PHILIP: That wasn't such a bad fish, Jonah.

JONAH (*rebaiting his hook*): Pah! A mosquito.

PHILIP: What do you expect here, Jonah, whales? The Gulf Stream doesn't come into Steeplechase in the winter time.

JONAH: Explain to me why we shouldn't buy Swanson's boat and go look for the Gulf Stream.

PHILIP: How do we know it's a good boat?

JONAH: How do we know it's a *bad* boat?

PHILIP: Every time anybody has sold me anything it's turned out bad.

JONAH: For a young man like you, your outlook is terrible.

PHILIP: I only tell you what happens to me.

JONAH: Aaah. . . . . Every day we buy things, and until we buy our coffins, none of them puts us into the grave.

PHILIP: Item two, we have not got five hundred dollars.

JONAH: In the coffee-pot in your room we have one hundred and ninety dollars. Am I wrong?

PHILIP: You are not wrong. But is one hundred and ninety dollars five hundred dollars? Answer that.

JONAH: Have we heard of the installment plan? In America everyone can be a king on the installment plan.

PHILIP: Has Swanson heard of the installment plan?

62

JONAH: Tomorrow he'll hear of it. Give me your objections.

PHILIP: Then we can't pay the installments and Swanson takes back the boat and we don't have a boat and we don't have a hundred and ninety dollars. This happened to me with a Stromberg-Carlson radio. Now when I want to hear the radio I go to the drug store on the corner and drink Coca-Colas.

JONAH: Look. Soon I will die, God forbid, and on my grave they'll put, "Here lies Jonah Goodman, a good son, a good husband, a good citizen, he worked like a horse all his life and he never did what he wanted to do." A little later you'll die and they'll change one or two particulars and put that on *your* grave. So?

PHILIP (*dreamily*): It's not so bad here. When I sit here I'm not the same man who cooks bad spaghetti ten hours a day in Angelina's Backyard, Italian cooking, table d'hôte, one dollar.

JONAH: You will be even less the same man off the coast of Cuba in the sunshine.

PHILIP: Jonah . . . . Angelina wants to marry me. (*There is a sudden silence and the air of good-fellowship is chilled.*)

JONAH: So?

PHILIP: I'm not anxious to marry her. . . . . (JONAH *cheers up.*) She reminds me of a woman who sings "Oh, promise me" in vaudeville.

JONAH: So that's easy. "No, Angelina," you say, "you don't click."

PHILIP: Then she'll fire me. It's not so easy to tell your boss you won't marry her.

JONAH: What does she want from you?

PHILIP: Once Angelina was married to a Greek. She likes Greeks.

JONAH: You got a problem.

PHILIP: Now I work ten hours a day; at night I'm a free man, I go fishing. If I get married I am half-boss, I stay in the kitchen day and night. Angelina buys meat that's almost bad, milk that's almost sour, vegetables that're almost rotten. When I send out a dinner to the dining room I feel like I have just printed a counterfeit dollar.

JONAH: Why is it nobody ever can work like he wants to work?

Now Harold Goff, flashily dressed, "strolls on atop the pier"; and very soon we get our first hint that this play may not be heading toward the comedic development we had expected. Even before Goff's arrival, as we begin to understand *why* these old men want to go, we laugh less. We have caught the implications of an unfair world around them. They *have* to extricate themselves from their circumstances; we would try to extricate ourselves from the same situation. As far as we are concerned, these two old men in their predicament are still out of focus, but they are not entirely funny any more. Even after the gangster opens up his threats and we feel certain that melodrama is imminent, we do not quite discard the feeling of understanding which is one of the accompaniments of comedy. Indeed, if the play as it goes on has enough verisimilitude in its portrayal of the social pressure and economic threat which force the old men to flee their circum-

stances, we may say—in spite of the differences between us—"*We might* have been in such a predicament ourselves."

It is in such ways that the comedies of today come
close to us: in the pattern of circumstance with
which contemporary characters have to make immediate adjustment—circumstances which we identify as our own. While the material of comedy is
always character-in-circumstance, the pattern of circumstance in which the characters arrange themselves is as new as each new generation. Today's
socioeconomic patterns together with today's philo-
sophic-religious patterns and the current patterns of
politics, government, art—all the composite present-
day patterns—are the matrix of circumstance in
which today's characters move. If the characters
move somewhat differently among their bewilder-
ments, somewhat more directly, more self-consciously, perhaps more analytically, it is because today has
brought out these qualities of personality. Even the
inner structure of individual personality is modified
by circumstances peculiar to this generation. What
other generation has had to make room for a world
war, an endemic depression, a league of nations, a
clipper fleet, a psychoanalytic technique, double-
feature movies, and a nation-wide hookup? "People

seem different today" just as a tree is different after its grain has been twisted in a storm or as inorganic crystals present a different juxtaposition of elements after they have passed through the crucible. Better, perhaps; perhaps not so good; but different. The same old material but stamped clear through with the trade-mark *Today*.

Sometimes these problems of today are so overwhelming that it seems impossible for the individual to extricate himself from them. The social forces become Fate, just as inexorably as the gods were Fate. When the individual cannot extricate himself, when he is completely defeated, no matter by what accumulation of comparative triviality, then his story is a tragedy, as we have seen. But many contemporary plays, although they contain tragic elements and show characters buffeted by social forces of today as cruelly as Destiny ever buffeted the heroes of an earlier day, still leave open a door of escape. In this open door—if it *is* open and not merely reflecting some light of hope from tired eyes—a question mark stands at attention: Can the characters pass through to ultimate adjustment? Perhaps that question mark is the brand of our generation. Can Anna and Chris, for instance, finally extricate themselves from the forces which appear to overpower them? If they can, then the play is not a tragedy. But if it is not a tragedy, then what shall we call a play so fraught with social consequence and so close to individual disaster? If playwrights and public are so unsure of the finality of things that most of our serious plays must be written and received with a note of indeterminateness which leaves no assurance of adjustment—merely a chance—then what kind of plays are we having? The academic labeler, feeling that he must paste some distinguishing mark beneath the title and unwilling to resort to the press agent's tactful term "a drama," adds an adjective and contrives the label "serious comedy."

This serious comedy, like all other varieties of comedy, admits the possibility of final adjustment for the individual. But some adjustment is such anguish for the individual, of such significance to society, that it requires the tension of will toward large ends which has heretofore been the mark of tragedy. We might think that we were in the presence of a new tragedy, except that the peculiar loftiness of tone which once distinguished tragedy is lacking, and the emotional grandeur eventuates in no sweeping catharsis, *and* defeat is not inevitable. So we have this realistic and very serious form of drama which is near the dividing-line of tragedy, with characters close to the edge of frustration. We in the audience, being human, watch with a peculiar fascination these characters as they pass before us—not marching to their inevitable doom, but balancing precariously on the tightrope of life as we ourselves know that life, sometimes all too well. We watch with the perspective which is the audience-response to comedy. We feel that maladjustment may not be permanent in the long run, neither theirs nor society's; and if maladjustment is not permanent, then life—or the play—is a comedy, however serious.

Indeterminate, with characters blocked by social forces yet given a chance of escape, Clifford Odets' *Awake and Sing* is a play of this kind. The Bergers are a Jewish family in New York. Ralph, a stock clerk in a silk house, turns over to his mother all his pay except five dollars a week. He is ardent, sensitive, protesting the *status quo*. His mother, Bessie Berger, has no soft sympathy for his ambitions or complaints; her own life has been hard and has granted her no quarry. His father, Myron, is vaguely sympathetic; his sister, Hennie, completely unmoved because her own troubles seem so much more immediate. But Jacob, his grandfather, understands and abets. The family speculate on what is to be expected of life, anyway. To Myron, it's a cakewalk. To Hennie, all it gets you is a four-car funeral. Jacob has other ideas. "If this life leads to a revolution it's a good life," he says. "Otherwise it's for nothing." But young Ralph protests: "It's crazy. All my life I want a pair of black and white shoes and can't get them. It's crazy."

The Bergers are used to weathering their economic insecurities, but now Hennie precipitates a new sort of insecurity when she admits her mother's suspicion that she's going to have a baby whose father cannot be found at the address where she has written to him. Bessie Berger falls to scheming at once. Sam Feinschreiber shall be invited to dinner tomorrow; by Saturday he and Hennie will be engaged. "He's a good boy only three years in the country and he speaks very nice." Hennie resents the trick but acquiesces. Moe Axelrod is told of the engagement but not of its cause—Moe Axelrod, friend of the family, former soldier who has lost a leg in the World War, one of the "disillusioned," who would like to marry Hennie himself but, "She wantsa see me crawl —my head on a plate she wants! A snowball in hell's got a better chance." So the engagement to Sam becomes a marriage, and old Jacob is deeply disgusted and shamed. More cause than ever to look to the salvaging of his grandson. "Ralph you don't make like you," he threatens the family. "Before you do it I'll die first. He'll find a girl. He'll go in a fresh world with her. This is a house? Marx said it—abolish such families." And Ralph does find a girl. He tells his grandfather about her.

> But she's got me! Boy, I'm telling you I could sing! Jake, she's like stars. She's so beautiful you look at her and cry! She's like French words! We went to the park the other night. Heard the last band concert.
>
> JACOB: Music. . . . .
>
> RALPH: It got cold and I gave her my coat to wear. We just walked along like that, see, without a word, see? I never was so happy in all my life. It got late. . . . . We just sat there. She looked at me—you know what I mean, how a girl looks at you—right in the eyes? "I love you," she says. I took her home. I wanted to cry. That's how I felt!

Her name is Blanche; she's poor; has no father or mother; lives with relations who are mean to her. Ralph's mother hears about her and doesn't like the idea of Ralph's falling in love; meets her and doesn't care for her, the more so because when Blanche takes Ralph she takes his sixteen dollars a week out of the house. Blanche is having trouble at home, where they "shove her around like a freight train"; but Ralph can't marry her without money. His rich uncle Morty who owns a dress business insists that his own success is no exception; Ralph can do as well if he wants to. Old Jacob doubts that.

No, Morty, I don't think. In a house like this he don't realize even the possibilities of life. Economics comes down like a ton of coal on the head. . . . . In my day the propaganda was for God. Now it's for success. A boy don't turn around without having shoved into him he should make a success.

MORTY: Pop, you're a comedian, a regular Charlie Chaplin.

JACOB: He dreams all night of fortunes. Why not? Don't it say in the movies he should have a personal steamship, pyjamas for fifty dollars a pair and a toilet like a monument? But in the morning he wakes up and for ten dollars he can't fix the teeth. . . . . (MORTY *laughs loud and long.*) Laugh, laugh . . . . tomorrow not.

Meanwhile Hennie's married life is not happy. The baby is always sick; Sam's attentions irritate her; she wishes she had gone with Moe. In a frenzy of exasperation she tells Sam that the baby is not his; but her mother and father quiet Sam's resentment and assure him that Hennie married him for love when she might have chosen much better. Suddenly Ralph realizes how crooked they all are. Moreover, his wages are cut, and Blanche is about to move to another city. Old Jacob sees the weight of the family situation caving in on Ralph. And one winter night the old man takes the dog to the roof for an airing; and slips off the roof. Not accidentally, as we know: he has felt that all he could give was his $3,000 insurance. This insurance becomes the family issue Moe tells Ralph the facts.

71

"Now you got wings, kid. Pop figured you could use it." But the family are in a wrangle over who really gets that money. Bessie thinks she's worked too hard all her years to be "treated like dirt."

The first two years I worked in a stocking factory for six dollars while Myron Berger went to law school. If I didn't worry about the family, who would? On the calendar it's a different place, but here without a dollar you don't look the world in the eye. Talk from now to next year—this is life in America.

RALPH: Then it's wrong. It don't make sense. If life made you this way, then it's wrong.

BESSIE: Maybe you wanted me to give up twenty years ago. Where would you be now? You'll excuse my expression—a bum in the park.

Ralph cannot accept life on such terms.

No, I see every house lousy with lies and hate. He said it, Grandpa—Brooklyn hates the Bronx. Smacked on the nose twice a day. But boys and girls can't get ahead like that, Mom. We don't want life printed on dollar bills, Mom.

BESSIE: So go out and change the world if you don't like it.

RALPH: I will! And why? 'Cause life's different in my head. Gimme the earth in my two hands. I'm strong.

And he begins to read old Jacob's books. He sets to work on his world: he'll get the boys in the warehouse to working together.

Get teams together all over. Spit on your hands and get to work. And with enough teams together maybe we'll get steam in the warehouse so our fingers don't freeze off. Maybe we'll fix it so life won't be printed on dollar bills.

Finally Hennie goes off with Moe, the disillusioned, the amoral, who has always craved her and who now sketches a future for her.

No more pins and needles in your heart, no snake juice squirted in your arm! The whole world's green grass and when you cry it's because you're happy. . . . . Mom can mind the kid. She'll go on forever, Mom. We'll send money back, and Easter eggs.

Ralph urges them to go. He looks at Hennie; he looks at his father, disappearing into the bedroom paring an apple.

RALPH: When I look at him, I'm sad. Let me die like a dog if I can't get more out of life.

HENNIE: Where?

RALPH: Right here in the house! My days won't be for nothing. Let Mom have the dough. I'll get along. Did Jake die for us to fight about nickels? "Awake and sing," he said. Right here he stood and said it. The night he died, I saw it like a thunderbolt. It saw he was dead and I was born! I swear to God I'm one week old. I want the whole city to hear it—fresh blood, arms. We got 'em. We're glad we're living.

MOE: I wouldn't trade you for two pitchers and an outfielder. Hold the fort!

RALPH: So long.

MOE: So long.

And so the final curtain comes down on *Awake and Sing* as Moe and Hennie go and Ralph "stands full and strong in the doorway seeing them off."

The audience feels no cozy sense of satisfaction at

this curtain, such as an audience may feel at the conclusion of another kind of play which can so readily be labeled "comedy"; no pleasant assurance, for instance, such as may be afforded by the final nostalgic moments of *Ah, Wilderness!* when Nat Miller and his wife speak of "youth's sweet-scented manuscript" as they "move quietly out of the moonlight, back into the darkness of the front parlor." This play *Awake and Sing* is quite another thing, and there is not much sweet-scentedness about the young Ralph, however "full and strong" he stands in the doorway to symbolize Odets' hope that the boy can build his world more to his grandfather's hopes. And many in the audience will doubtless exclaim, in varying tones of meaning, "Propaganda!" Surely; Odets is the first to nod assent; he intends it that way. But if he has transcended his message—perhaps indeed if he has succeeded in giving a message at all—he has let us look upon real characters in a real situation, and the picture of Ralph in the doorway stays with us as of someone we have actually known, and we wonder what happens to him afterward. The playwright, after the manner of today's uncertitudes, has not given the full answer; he has merely pointed the possibility. Ralph stands in the doorway. The open door, we must conclude, of possible adjustments. Moe Axelrod, long before the play beings, has made a sort of makeshift adjustment to life, and at the end he goes on toward one definite kind of "happiness." Hennie goes with him, but Hennie has been defeated all along the line; the barriers of economics in the crowded home have been too much for her; and now in her apparent escape she is just as uncertain, as maladjusted, as always. Yet the end of the play does seem to give some promise that Ralph may, "right here in the house," surmount his circumstances. He has become, fully, old Jacob's grandson. Jacob chose death which for the old man was merely a negative form of adjustment; he found final achievement for himself in making it possible (as he thought) for Ralph to use the insurance money to go on with. Of course what he really passed on to Ralph was something more important: Ralph has a chance now to escape by means of his own resources, the realization of which is his true inheritance from Jacob. Life takes on meaning for him, and his understanding is a first step in his adjustment.

Awake and Sing, besides exemplifying this sort of play which may be called comedy because of the possibility of adjustment, illustrates another tendency in our theater today: our current plays are likely to deal with the American family. Even *What a Life*, though so far from serious that some will call it farce instead of comedy, deals with an urgent phase of family affairs, the school life of the adolescent. *Ah, Wilderness!*, plainly a sentimental comedy, looks into the psychology of the adolescent in a family frame that includes for good measure the spinster and the bachelor. *The Gentle People*, though its solution is frankly melodrama, is built on one man's escape from a nagging wife and on the "rescue" of his daughter, and on the other man's hope of escape from a marriage with a woman who will "boss" him. In fact, whether in farce, melodrama, or the more obviously serious forms, the attention of both established and aspiring writers seems to be fixed on some phase of the family in American life. It is interesting to find that even in the Charles H. Sergel national contest, which in 1939 called for a one-act comedy dealing with American life, a vast majority of the manuscripts submitted (probably over 90 per cent) treated the family scene, most of them emphasizing some angle of the parent-child relationship.

Why, one asks, does the stage serve as a focus lens for the problem of the family today? Probably because most of the larger problems which beset society all bear in on the family. They affect us where we live, which for most of us is in family groups. For example, unemployment, old-age insurance, farm subsidy, would mean little to us except as *some of our own* are affected by the need of a job, a pension, a crop. The current problems have been years in accumulating—at least since the beginning of the new century—and in the process they have changed the very nature of family life. Women have been going out of the home to work until now we have ceased to blink when sociologists flaunt their statistics showing how many women act as whole or part-time breadwinners. We have accepted the fact that the major part of the housework is said to be done "outside the home"; that one out of every five meals is eaten away from home; that most of the family clothes are made in factories. We take it for granted that members of the family spend far less time together than they used to spend; that children are not so strictly disciplined; that the family car is as likely to be a disruptive as an integrative factor in family life. We agree that it is no longer a disgrace for a man frankly to be unable to furnish the entire support for his family; no longer questionable for a woman to want a profession or job of her own even though necessity does not demand it of her. So many factors are forcing change in the family setup that we now think in terms of change instead of in terms of stable patterns. The authors of *Middletown* assert that "the cumulating rapidity of recent social change" widens in something like a geometric ratio "the gap between things that were 'right' yesterday and those that make sense to the new generation today." Most of the contemporary perplexities therefore have seemed to walk right into the home, through front door or back door, and made themselves part of the family's continual struggle for adjustment.

It appears only reasonable, then, for the theater to pick up current problems at the point where they seem most personal; where they may thwart youth, defeat marriage, disrupt the home. Thus in *Awake and Sing* the family are stifled by the general problem of economic insecurity which they are powerless to do anything about, though some of them—Ralph in particular—see their way to do something about their own immediate problem and in doing so suggest an answer, an "adjustment," which may possibly work for the larger group. They become leverage for the heavier, less personal problems of society.

Sidney Howard's *The Silver Cord* deals with another stratum of society, dramatizing a family problem just as acute to the individuals concerned, all of

them of the comfortably "well-to-do" class. Among
the earlier of the plays to set the contemporary mood
for dealing with an old family situation, Howard's
drama is built on the theme of a mother's domina-
tion of her sons. We know that Robert's ultimate relationship to his young fiancée, Hester, who has
come to the Phelps home to spend the holidays, will
depend upon his mother's acceptance of the girl.
We know that the future of David and his young
wife, Christina, whom he has just brought home from
Europe, may also depend upon the will of the
mother. Even at the tea table, when Mrs. Phelps is
being charmingly cordial to the other women, she
manages to make them feel apologetically in the
way and to make the sons feel that they have in-
truded an unnecessary element into the perfect happiness of an "unselfish and motherly" mother who
lives for her sons. Later, when Mrs. Phelps learns
from Christina that David and Christina expect to
continue their work in New York, he as an architect
and she as a research biologist, we see the mother
begin her determined maneuverings to keep David
in his home town, building houses for a new sub-
division, while Christina "if she must have a career"
can spend odd hours in the local hospital. With
"loving" but insinuating questions, Mrs. Phelps next

79

makes Robert begin to doubt Hester's love and then to doubt his own love for the girl; can his feeling for Hester after all be so intense a loyalty and devotion as he has always felt for his mother? And if not . . . . ? If not, a breaking of the engagement, which naturally ensues. Christina sees through all of the maneuverings; in honest sympathy for Hester and in stubborn devotion to the life which she and David have begun to build together, she demands that she and David shall leave the house the next morning when Hester leaves. But Hester, bewildered and desperate, will not wait for morning to usher her neatly out of Mrs. Phelps's house. She tries to escape at night and falls through the ice on the pond, being rescued by David against his mother's wild protests that he will catch pneumonia. When the physician arrives to care for Hester and for Mrs. Phelps, who is having one of her "bad spells," he takes occasion to tell Robert that the mother's heart attacks are part of her determination to hold her sons entirely for herself. Under the impact of this revelation and Christina's insistence that he cut loose from his mother and lead an adult life, David leaves with his wife. But Robert cannot extricate himself from his mother's self-love; he is forever bound by intricately woven cords of selfishness.

Comedy? The labeler will say so, because the door swings open for David and Christina. They escape, whole and determined, larger characters than they were at the play's beginning. Hester, too, may ultimately escape, though her life seems warped and twisted for the present. Robert will never escape, at least while his mother lives. He is as mother-bound as Charlie in O'Neill's *Strange Interlude*. Robert's one chance, and that a slight one, is that after his mother's death life may jolt him free. For the mother there is also defeat, even though she has half-succeeded in her schemes, because she has kept her younger son at the price of unremitting vigilance over him and over her own selfishness. Serious comedy about the family; about today's family in which a young wife must fight for her heritage as a person, as an individual with work of her own to be done, at the same time that she fights for her prerogatives as a wife. When Christina wins out, many of the audience win with her, perhaps even those who feel themselves to be defeated. They see that doors which for centuries have only opened *in* may with pushing enough also open *out*. There is a measure of vicarious achievement in seeing other feet walk through newly opened doors. The onlooker realizes that society always walks slowly, *en masse*. He himself may furnish some of the lag, but the column moves forward before his eyes. Some of the best pace-setters—although not the earliest pioneers—have always been on the stage.

In George Kelly's *Craig's Wife*, another of the earlier plays—it is more than a decade since Chrystal Herne's photographic impersonation of Harriet Craig made thousands of American women see the woman-next-door as real as life—it is the wife who tries to dominate. Walter Craig is walled away from his friends, blocked in his business advancement, stifled in his own personal happiness, by a wife who insists on misconstruing actions and doubting motives —his and his friends'. When his aunt, Miss Austen, manages to show him the real situation, Walter has to choose between his accustomed security and affection and his own personal integrity. He chooses integrity and makes a complete break with wife and domestic setup. Again, "serious comedy" says the labeler, though the play skirts tragedy because the wife is left alone and will probably remain alone. As the aunt has said, "People who live to themselves, Harriet, are generally left to themselves," which is a predicament having about it more of death than of life. True, Harriet is defeated; but the mood of her defeat is not the mood of grandeur such

as rises from the defeat of great characters; it is the
mood of futility which follows the raveling-out of
mediocrity. Nor does Harriet Craig's defeat dominate the play. The play is dominated by Walter
Craig's escape. The end of the action may be indeterminate, but Walter's character gives a hint—even
an assurance—for tomorrow. The playwright has
not been afraid to look "realistically" at a type of
woman who threatens the success of matrimony.
Kelly again, in a play more indubitably comedy, evi-
denced his willingness to draw a sharp line between
the traditional sentimentalities of family "sacrifice"
and the actuality of a man threatened with being
submerged by them. Indeed, the theme of *Daisy
Mayme*, worked out pleasantly as it is, is italicized
unmistakably. It is Daisy Mayme Plunkett herself
who, by action as well as words, shows Cliff Met-
tinger the way to a new emancipation.

> You can do it; but you've got to get over all your illusions
> first—especially your illusions about your own people. That's
> what *I* had to do. And I've been a happy woman ever since.
> Ever since I woke up to the fact that they'll let the willing
> horse pull the load.

No one recently has looked at a family with more
relentless realism that Lillian Hellman in *The Little
Foxes*. And that she chooses the spring of 1900 as the

time of her play does not mean that she is any the less of today in her analysis; indeed, it is in part *because* of the time of the action that she can point what she has to imply about our own day. The particular "little foxes that spoil the vines" are the members of the Hubbard family; but we are left with the feeling that it is not only at the beginning of the century that "our vines have tender grapes."

The story of the Hubbards is the story of a new way of life foisted upon an older way of life, or a new way perhaps growing out of the older way; a ruthless, crude certainty out of a sensitive, romantic uncertainty. In 1900 Birdie Hubbard, a woman approaching forty "with a pretty, well-bred, faded face," is an echo of the Old South of plantation aristocracy and *noblesse oblige;* she moves through the new ways like a remembered refrain which recalls the dignity and grace and pride of less hurried days but loses its identity among the strident notes of incompassionate new industries and insatiable new greeds. Birdie knows her place among these Hubbards. When she married Oscar, she literally married into the family, so different from her own with its stately seat at Lionnet. There is Ben Hubbard, the unmarried brother, in his mid-fifties, using each new opportunity as a bridge from yesterday's success to tomorrow's, not caring upon whose backs the piles of his bridges rest. There is Regina, handsome, self-assured, shrewd; able to hold her own with her brothers while her husband, Horace Giddens, is off at Johns Hopkins being treated for a serious heart ailment. Horace too has been a successful man, president of the bank, influential in the community; but he belongs to the old school, his ways and his values are outside the Hubbard ken. Oscar Hubbard, Birdie's husband, has less finesse than his brother Ben or his sister Regina, and probably more cruelty in a dull, indifferent way. Leo, the son of Oscar and Birdie, has the weakness of both without his mother's sensitivity or his father's stolid determination. The contrast in the younger generation is made between him and Alexandra, daughter of Regina and Horace, who is "a very pretty, rather delicate looking girl of seventeen." The thoroughbred strain is dominant in Alexandra, but through most of the play her mother and her uncles confuse docility with weakness; eventually they can no more manage Alexandra than they can change themselves.

When the curtain goes up, the Hubbards have come to a big moment in their careers. Not that their careers have been without other big moments. They have gone far since their great-grandfather

85

came south, for he was not, as Ben says, "an aristo-
crat like Birdie's": he went into trade. The family
made enough money eventually to buy Lionnet,
Birdie's plantation home. Today the Hubbard sons
still own Lionnet, but now it is merely one among
their many properties; for three generations Hubbards have been buying, selling, using political and
economic pressure to intrench themselves. Now, as
we first see them, they are consummating a big
transaction with a Mr. Marshall from the North; instead of shipping cotton north to be manufactured,
they will have the manufacturing brought south to
take advantage of the cheap southern labor. Profits
should be enormous. After the deal is sealed with a
toast, Leo and Alexandra drive Mr. Marshall to his
train while the rest of the Hubbards, set off by Regina, break into animated discussion of what they
will do with their new fortunes. "Daydream stuff,"
whereby the dramatist breaks open these characters
so that we see the springs of motivation which feed
their subsequent actions. Regina knows very well
what she wants; she will move to Chicago and make
herself a part of the best society—a leading part;
there could be nothing halfway or uncalculated even
in Regina's dreams. Ben already has most of the
things that he wants, except more money, but he

thinks that he might buy up a stable—"the sport of kings, why not the sport of Hubbards?" Oscar, never an inventive genius in love or business, will take his pleasure in "watching the bricks grow" in the new factory, and then maybe he and Birdie might take a little trip. Birdie too knows very well what she wants; Birdie who, we remember, is not really a Hubbard at all; Birdie who seems always to be backing into tomorrow with her eyes clinging fondly to yesterday. The others are willing to humor her for a moment, to the extent of letting her voice her wish in the midst of their own more important desires.

OSCAR (*indulgently*): What would you like?

BIRDIE: *Two* things. Two things I'd like most.

REGINA: Two! I should like a thousand. You are modest, Birdie.

BIRDIE (*warmly, delighted with the unexpected interest*): I should like to have Lionnet back. I know you own it now, but I'd like to see it fixed up again, the way Mama and Papa had it. Every year it used to get a nice coat of paint—Papa was very particular about the paint—and the lawn was so smooth all the way down to the river, with the trims of zinnias and red-feather plush. And the figs and blue little plums and the scuppernongs—(*Smiles. Turns to* REGINA.) The organ is still there and it wouldn't cost much to fix. We could have parties for Zan, the way Mama used to have for me.

BEN: That's a pretty picture, Birdie. Might be a most pleasant way to live. (*Dismissing* BIRDIE.) What do you want, Regina?

87

BIRDIE (*very happily, not noticing that they are no longer listening to her*): I could have a cutting garden. Just where Mama's used to be. Oh, I do think we could be happier there. Papa used to say that *nobody* had ever lost their temper at Lionnet, and *nobody* ever would. Papa would never let anybody be nasty-spoken or mean. No, sir. He just didn't like it.

BEN: What do you want, Regina?

REGINA: I'm going to Chicago. And when I'm settled there and know the right people and the right things to buy—because I certainly don't now—I shall go to Paris and buy them. (*Laughs.*) I'm going to leave you and Oscar to count the bricks.

BIRDIE: Oscar. Please let me have Lionnet back.

OSCAR (*to* REGINA): You are serious about moving to Chicago?

BEN: She is going to see the great world and leave us in the little one. Well, we'll come and visit you and meet all the great and be proud to think you are our sister.

REGINA (*gaily*): Certainly. And you won't even have to learn to be subtle, Ben. Stay as you are. You will be rich and the rich don't have to be subtle.

Thus the timid Birdie has little chance to get her other wish fully into the conversation, though she finally does let them know—if they are listening— that she would like Oscar to stop shooting; "I mean, so much." But the family have serious things to talk about. Oscar lays before Regina the exact terms of the contract with Marshall. Marshall is to bring the factory to the cotton, taking advantage of the cheap labor which the Hubbards have the power to provide; and he is to pay four hundred thousand dollars for 49 per cent of the stock. The Hubbards are to pay two hundred twenty-five thousand dollars for 51 per cent. They have offered to permit Regina to take up one-third of that stock, but it is imperative that the money be forthcoming at once. Why doesn't Horace answer their letters? Regina will take care of Horace; the money will be forthcoming. Immediately. She will send Alexandra to bring Horace home; he will be touched to have the girl come for him; Regina will even send him a message about missing him herself. So the brothers need have no concern over the seventy-five thousand dollars; *but* she will take 40 per cent of the Hubbard stock in return for her third of the investment. The brothers protest, but uselessly. Regina is a Hubbard and they know it; she has seen their eagerness to keep control of the company within the family, and this is her price. They must make the best of it; they do. Now Oscar allows himself another fancy. Leo and Alexandra were a handsome pair going off together; it might be a nice thing if Leo should marry his cousin and so keep the entire fortune in the family. Ben agrees, and so, apparently, does Regina. Birdie, however, is horrified, frightened. She loves Alexandra and she knows Leo. How can fluttering, useless hands beat back the inevitable? But she tries, later, after the young people have returned. Alone with Alexandra for a moment, she warns her about the marriage plans. Alexandra only laughs. She would never think of such an arrangement! Unfortunately Oscar has slipped back into the room in time to overhear the girl's remark. He stands there a moment until Alexandra has started upstairs to pack for her trip. Then, "as Birdie quickly attempts to pass him, he slaps her hard, across the face." Involuntarily Birdie cries out and Alexandra runs down the stairs to see what has happened. But Birdie assures her it is nothing; she merely turned her ankle. Alexandra is not reassured. As her aunt goes, the girl "stands on the stairs looking after her as if she were puzzled and frightened." Thus in an incident the playwright again builds the play's time-dimension, for Birdie's reaction in covering Oscar's quick cruelty is born, we know, of many similar incidents stretching back toward those early days when he married her for the Lionnet cotton. And Alexandra's puzzled concern is premonition of a future in which she must understand her own family. The Hubbards may cow their women; but in this incident the defenseless women seem to stand as a threat—gentle, inarticulate as yet, but relentless—to the Hubbard strength.

Horace and Alexandra do not reach home on the night they are expected and the next morning finds Ben and Oscar at Regina's house, irritable over the delay. The money is needed at once. Leo comes from the bank and mentions to Oscar that he has seen in Uncle Horace's safe-deposit box Union Pacific bonds to the value of eighty-eight thousand dollars. Just lying there among some useless mementos—perhaps forgotten, since Horace looks into his box only once in six months, if that often. Now if Leo had that much stock—But Oscar has begun to ask questions which steer the conversation toward Leo's future and the fortune which might be his if, for instance, he could himself buy into the new mills. Gradually Leo gets the point; the "borrowing" of the bonds is arranged, and Ben is acquainted with this new way of meeting the payment to Marshall.

Now at last Horace and Alexandra have arrived. Horace is obviously a very ill man; Alexandra and the old colored servant Addie arrange his medicines within reach of his wheel chair even before they call Regina who, as soon as she is alone with her husband, begins the recriminations and innuendos which have been her customary attack upon him. Apparently his life has never suited her, and she is not pleased by his long stay in the hospital, his reluctant and unhurried return. There are heated words both ways, but Horace recovers his composure. He has so short a time to live; he has made his peace with life and with the fact of death. Now he is tired and would not discuss the business which Regina feels to be so pressing. But she insists. She does not note her husband's drawn face—or does she? At any rate, she calls in her brothers. She knows that they will help her. But Ben is suddenly solicitous for Horace. The business can wait. They have provided another way of meeting that payment; Oscar is leaving for Chicago this very evening. Regina is stunned; she sees the fortune slipping from her clever fingers, and without adequate explanation. She is furious with her brothers, and they part in bitterness. Horace is quietly amused—at last Regina and Ben have had a major quarrel! Regina is coldly incensed. She tells Horace that she understands his reluctance to see her succeed where he must fail, to know she is living when he must die. She has never had what she wanted of him, but she is going to get it now: her freedom, her chance to go ahead at her own gait. Thus goaded, Horace wearily but with determination speaks his mind.

I'm sick of you, sick of this house, sick of my life here. I'm sick of your brothers and their dirty tricks to make a dime. There must be better ways of getting rich than cheating niggers on a pound of bacon. Why should I give you the money? (*Very angrily.*) To pound the bones of this town to make dividends for you to spend? You wreck the town, you and your brothers, *you* wreck the town and live on it. Not me. Maybe it's easy for the dying to be honest. But it's not my fault I'm dying. (ADDIE *enters, stands at door quietly.*) I'll do no more harm now. I've done enough. I'll die my own way. And I'll do it without making the world any worse. I leave that to you.

REGINA (*looks up at him slowly, calmly*): I hope you die. I hope you die soon. (*Smiles.*) I'll be waiting for you to die.

The two weeks that Oscar is away on his trip are not unpleasant days for Horace. Old Addie looks after his needs; Alexandra and Birdie play the piano for him. One sunny morning the three of them—he and Birdie and Alexandra—are having a little impromptu party together—elderberry wine and cakes along with Birdie's gay and rather tender chatter. She likes telling Alexandra how good the girl's father has been to her all these years. And then the wine begins to unlock reminiscences.

Mama used to give me elderberry wine when I was a little girl. For hiccoughs. (*Laughs.*) You know, I don't think people get hiccoughs any more. Isn't that funny? (BIRDIE *laughs.* HORACE *and* ALEXANDRA *laugh.*) I used to get hiccoughs just when I shouldn't have.

ADDIE (*nods*): And nobody gets growing pains no more.

That is funny. Just as if there was some style in what you get. One year an ailment's stylish and the next year it ain't.

BIRDIE (*turns*): I remember. It was my first big party, at Lionnet I mean, and I was so excited, and there I was with hiccoughs and Mama laughing. (*Softly. Looking at carafe.*) A big party, a lovely dress from Mr. Worth in Paris, France, and hiccoughs. (*Pours drink.*) My brother pounding me on the back and Mama with the elderberry bottle, laughing at me. Everybody was on their way to come and I was such a ninny, hiccoughing away. (*Drinks.*) You know, that was the first day I ever saw Oscar Hubbard. The Ballongs were selling their horses and he was going there to buy. He passed and lifted his hat—we could see him from the window—and my brother, to tease Mama, said maybe we should have invited the Hubbards to the party. He said Mama didn't like them because they kept a store, and he said that was old-fashioned of her. (*Her face lights up.*) And then, and *then*, I saw Mama angry for the first time in my life. She said that wasn't the reason. She said she was old-fashioned, but not that way. She said she was old-fashioned enough not to like people who killed animals they couldn't use, and who made their money charging awful interest to poor, ignorant niggers and cheating them on what they bought. She was very angry, Mama was. I had never seen her face like that. And then suddenly she laughed and said, "Look, I've frightened Birdie out of the hiccoughs." (*Her head drops. Then softly.*) And so she had. They were all gone.

Birdie has opened the past not only to herself but to Alexandra. "Why did you marry Uncle Oscar?" Birdie doesn't know, really. Except that Ben Hubbard wanted Lionnet and "Oscar married it for him." But reminiscence is too strong a draught for Birdie; she tempers it with more elderberry wine. Addie cautions her that she will have another of her headaches, whereupon Birdie turns sharply to the old servant.

I've never had a headache in my life. (*Begins to cry hysterically.*) You know it as well as I do. (*Turns to* ALEXANDRA.) I never had a headache, Zan. That's a lie they tell for me. I drink. All by myself, in my own room, by myself, I drink. Then, when they want to hide it, they say, "Birdie's got a headache again"—

She is afraid now that Alexandra won't like her any more; and then, when the girl says that she will always love her, Birdie turns and speaks furiously.

Well, don't. Don't love me. Because in twenty years you'll be just like me. They'll do all the same things to you.

A prophecy, a premonition, a warning? Alexandra is not ready to know—yet. But with Horace it is different. He knows. So when Alexandra has taken Birdie home, he speaks firmly to Addie. She must look after Alexandra when he is gone; must stand up for her against whatever threatens. As for Addie herself, he tells her where he has left seventeen hundred dollars in bills for her. Now Regina comes in and promptly orders Horace back to his own rooms. But he has something to say to his wife; she might as well sit down and listen. He has chanced to send for his safe-deposit box and has discovered that the negotiable bonds are missing. He has pieced together the story of Leo's theft, understands Oscar's trip to Chicago. But he doesn't intend to do anything about the theft. It can pass as a loan from Regina to her brothers—because that eighty-eight thousand dollars is *all* he is leaving Regina. The rest of the estate goes to Alexandra; he is about to draw up a new will, has sent for his lawyer. So long as he lives he will say that he lent her brothers that money. . . . . *So long as he lives.* . . . . Regina begins to attack him bitterly—calculatingly. The argument is too much for Horace; pain overtakes him. She pays no attention to his groping for his medicine, his dropping it, his gasping whispered request that Addie be called to bring the other bottle from upstairs. Realizing that his wife will give him no help, he makes a desperate effort to get up the stairs. Only after he has fallen on the landing, out of view, does Regina summon aid.

While servants scurry for the doctor and Horace is making his last fight for life upstairs, Regina takes her last stand against her brothers. They are all there now, all the Hubbards—Regina, Ben, Oscar—even Leo, who has had a hurried moment in which to let the other men know that Horace has discovered the theft of the bonds. Calm in the midst of their consternation, Regina has explained the motive of Horace's silence. The brothers are again relieved. They are sorry for Regina, but they themselves are safe. Regina has an answer to that.

Safe while Horace lives, but I don't think Horace will live. And if he doesn't live I shall want seventy-five per cent in exchange for the bonds.

The brothers laugh at her. Let them laugh; it is 75 per cent or jail. While they are trying to discount this threat, Alexandra and Addie come slowly down the stairs. Horace is dead. But Regina, almost immediately, is pushing her advantage with Ben and Oscar. In the morning she will tell Judge Simmes about Leo. She will also tell her story to Mr. Marshall, who will call off the deal rather than be involved in scandal. She would prefer to hush everything up, on her own terms; but she is prepared either way. Oscar leaves angrily, but Ben accepts the loss.

. . . . One loses today and wins tomorrow. I said to myself, years of planning and I get what I want. Then I don't get it. But I'm not discouraged. The century's turning, the world is open. Open for people like you and me. Ready for us, waiting for us. After all this is just the beginning. There are hundreds of Hubbards sitting in rooms like this throughout the country.

97

All their names aren't Hubbard, but they are all Hubbards and they will own this country some day.

Ben Hubbard is speaking in the spring of 1900. Is the playwright speaking, through him, for what she sees today?

Alone with Alexandra, Regina is now ready to listen to the girl. But Alexandra no longer has anything to say. Not anything that matters; she knows what she must do. She has finally seen her family as they are—her mother, her uncles, her father, herself; and it is what she has seen that makes her so sure of the course she must take. She is going away from her mother. Because she wants to go and because she knows that her father would want her to go. If her mother refuses, it won't make any difference. Well, Regina decides wearily, she will not stop her; too many people used to make *her* do too many things. No, she will not compel Alexandra to stay.

ALEXANDRA: You couldn't, Mama, because I want to leave here. As I've never wanted anything in my life before. Because now I understand what Papa was trying to tell me. (*Pause.*) All in one day: Addie said there were people who ate the earth and other people who stood around and watched them do it. And just now Uncle Ben said the same thing. Really, he said the same thing. (*Tensely.*) Well, tell him for me, Mama, I'm not going to stand around and watch you do it. Tell him I'll be fighting as hard as he'll be fighting (*Rises*) some place where people don't just stand around and watch.

With this speech we are ready for the final curtain.
Or are we? Just for an instant comes a "moment of
final suspense" before the curtain is signaled down.
Regina, on the stairway, pauses, turns to look down
upon her young daughter. She speaks to her very
quietly, very appealingly though seemingly matter-
of-factly. ". . . . Would you like to come and talk to
me, Alexandra? Would you—would you like to sleep
in my room tonight?" And as Alexandra takes a step
toward her and says, "Are you afraid, Mama?" we
catch a sudden breath. Is Alexandra wavering, sur-
rendering perhaps? Just when she has her foot firmly
in the door to escape, to adjustment? But as Regina,
not answering—perhaps more than half-sure that
Alexandra will be following her—moves out of sight,
Addie comes to the girl's side, presses her arm—
Addie, who had been commissioned by Horace to
see that Alexandra did not waver. We are sure now
which way Alexandra is going; and the curtain is
down.

Of course we do not know just where Alexandra
Hubbard goes after the final curtain. We know only
that she is of a new generation, with some of the old
way and some of the new way in her, and the best of
each. Somewhere along the line she will find adjustment; at least she will be building steadily toward

it. Her father did not find adjustment; death opened a final and not unwelcome door, but he only partly escaped defeat. Probably a kind of curtailed adjustment for Ben and Oscar; they are the strong of the earth, and the strong win out over the thoroughbreds like Birdie who never had a chance. For Regina? She too is strong; stronger than her brothers; so strong that success may only bring defeat because, when she realizes finally that Alexandra has no need or place for her, she will stand very much alone. And know it. Success for her is at best a brittle achievement. But we feel that Alexandra's spirit will continue to elude the hand of circumstance. Her future may be uncertain as to events; but having once understood *when* to escape from *what*, and *why*, her own integrity will become her surety.

This play, within the conventional restrictions of a theater-piece though it is, seems somehow to have the dimensions of a novel—characters fully drawn, circumstances in perspective. Behind the main action of the play looms the shadow of "social forces" which our day can see more realistically than could those who lived in the day of which the playwright writes. Behind this play about the Hubbards there seems to be another play on a grander scale, depicting the rise of industrialism sowing its own seeds of

future confusions, ... and a play about the ineffi-
cacy of all those who, like Birdie, do not understand
the forces which threaten their extinction, ... and
a play about the dawn of some new day when youth
will begin life again "some place where people don't
just stand around and watch." But those other plays
which we sense, towering above the Hubbards, are
also plays about people, about multiplied numbers
of individuals, *whom we see through the Hubbards.*
Characters. Essentially there is no other material
to make a play about. Characters sufficiently like
ourselves, one way or another, so that their triumph
over circumstance or their defeat by circumstance—
the interpenetration of themselves and circumstance
—matters a great deal to us.

Other playwrights have been indicating this tendency to comment upon the present by means of
scenes from another day. Sometimes they do it quite
obviously, as when in *Knickerbocker Holiday* Maxwell
Anderson dramatizes what he seems to consider a
danger in the present-day setup by telling a story of
the regime of Peter Stuyvesant in old New York.
The chief enjoyment of this production may have
sprung from the music and the lyrics, and from the
skill of Walter Huston in making Peter come alive
as a character; but many in the audience—chiefly

partisans, to be sure—felt that young Brom Broeck appeared more of a national type than he could have seemed if he had worn the clothes and spoken the catch phrases of the nineteen-thirties. They chuckled and applauded when Brom told Peter that he, Brom, was the first of a new people, the American people, who were incapable of regimentation, with whom dictatorship could never succeed; and their laughter indicated that they caught Anderson's point when, at the finish, Peter looked out upon the audience (who represented posterity) and assured them that

> All characters and all events
> Incorporated in our play
> Are fictional in every way.

This somewhat unorthodox "musical" pried frankly, through the past, into a controversial and even rather personal question of the day, though often with good-natured hilarity.

In more serious fashion Robert E. Sherwood's *Abe Lincoln in Illinois* speaks for contemporary America through the scenes, and frequently through the very words, of yesterday. When Lincoln debates with Douglas, he talks about the textile workers of Massachusetts in phrases which might have been lifted from a this-week's journal of current opinion. The effect of his speech upon the audience is to underscore a present-day situation of which the audience is already aware. Probably no one in contemporary life could speak with so much authority on this problem of today as Lincoln spoke in the words of yesterday, because he speaks as a prophet who is felt by many to have vindicated his authority to speak.

The indeterminateness of what the labeler calls "serious comedy" marks the conclusion of Sherwood's play, as indeed uncertainty has seemed to be the keynote of the life it depicts. Abe Lincoln in Salem would like to go to Springfield to the legislature, but is it the move for him? Is he cut out for a political career? He goes, not quite sure; and he stays, no more sure. He finds it difficult to vote on many questions and impossible to lead out on many of the issues in which he believes because there are always arguments on the other side, always extenuating circumstances. Even on the question of slavery, the issue is complicated by states' rights, and Lincoln insists upon withholding opinion which may precipitate hasty action. Later, when he accepts the nomination for the presidency, he does it with misgivings; when the election returns are coming in, he is as fearful of being elected as of being defeated. In personal affairs he frequently seems no more certain.

103

On the very day of his expected marriage to Mary Todd, he calls off the wedding; and he wanders for some months in the wilderness of Indiana and Illinois, only coming back to the marriage by a circuitous route of decision. But throughout these uncertainties, both private and public, the playwright indicates the rise of a growing spire of certainty: the first rights of man are the "human" rights—justice, truth, freedom—a few inalienable heritages a man dare give himself to maintain. With each succeeding scene of the play, the spire of certainty rises through the increasing uncertainties which surround him. In the last scene we see Lincoln on the platform of the train which is to take him to Washington to assume his duties as president of the United States. In simple, short sentences he speaks to his friends and neighbors. He is not sure what lies ahead; he is not sure that he is the man to lead the American people; but he is sure that *somehow* the American people must find their way to maintain their essential democracy.

As he finishes speaking to them and bids them good-bye, the band strikes up "John's Brown's Body"; the cheering grows to an uproar; the voices of the crowd are raised in the words of the song, until all are singing the final line as the curtain comes down. Thus the real "tag" of the play is not a spoken line but the familiar words of a song, "His truth goes marching on." A solemn note, a triumphant song, *but an indeterminate ending. Will* democracy go marching on? The question rises not alone from the play but from the audience. In fact, in this play the audience is more than ordinarily a part of the play. They have brought details of the Lincoln story and their feeling for the Lincoln legend into the theater with them. They have filled in the background for the scenes on the stage, and in their memories they have carried the rest of the story to its conclusion. But how will the story ultimately conclude? Against the background of American hopes and traditions and determinations, this larger-than-life figure points toward democracy's uncertain future, of which the contemporary audience is more aware than any audience to whom Lincoln might have spoken in his own day. The manner in which Raymond Massey the actor realizes the popular picture which almost every American schoolboy has built up of Lincoln adds materially to the impression audiences get that here is a prophet of the past speaking to them directly.

Yet many who feel this way will wonder at the label "comedy" for a drama about Lincoln. They

have, some of them, grown up with the thought that
the career of Abraham Lincoln was tragic. Tragic,
yes, according to the connotation of that word in the
average mind. But is it possible to write a genuine
tragedy about one whom martyrdom has only en-
hanced, enlivened, authenticated? He died; but he
died grandly without defeat. His was no continuing
maladjustment but an apparent rising over circumstance to what the present-day audience considers a
triumph and with which the audience chooses to
identify itself. In such a mood one may say that it
is not possible to write a real tragedy, as it would be
impossible to write a tragedy around the character
of Robert E. Lee, who though he surrendered as a
soldier was both before and after Appomattox triumphant as an individual. We feel that he, like Lincoln, carried the sorrows of half the nation in his
heart and that his plans for the reconstruction of the
South in terms of education and agriculture soared
aboved the technicality of political defeat. Difficult
to build a real tragedy around the leader of that lost
cause or around the leader of the cause that won;
but it is possible that some younger playwright some
day may be able to fashion a tragedy around the
career of Woodrow Wilson, may be able in that
other American character to show dramatically the

individual battling to his inevitable personal catastrophe. The "Fourteen Points" . . . . the armistice . . . . acclaiming, adulating crowds . . . . the Versailles Treaty . . . . and then. . . . .

Between *Abe Lincoln in Illinois* and *The Road to Rome*, produced in 1927, Sherwood has gone a considerable distance in attitude. The earlier play was more akin to a type as old at least as Bernard Shaw's *Caesar and Cleopatra* of the nineties, a type which had as its thesis the fact that the characters of history were human beings like the rest of us, responsive to ordinary human impulses—with emphasis on the "ordinary." Many of these plays through the first decades of the century posed their historical characters against the screen of the latest historian's research and the latest psychologist's analysis; and many of them seemed to say, with a wisecracking satisfaction, "See how much smarter *we* are today than *they* were then!" Now, however, our playwrights seem to be looking back with a thought, or at least a guess, that some of those who survived anonymity in their own generation must have known a good deal about the essentials of living. These writers do not turn to such characters of history for enlightenment about another day so much as they turn to them for enlightenment about our own day

107

and for suggestions, perhaps, as to how we may meet our present perplexities. For we feel that we can see the "newness" of our own problems only as we sense the continuing human problem which binds the generations together; we know when we are dealing with the accouterments of modernity only as we know when we are dealing with the ongoing struggle of man to find and free himself.

Among these plays about yesterday, one might say that none is more of the present mood than *Family Portrait*, by Lenore Coffee and William Joyce Cowen. Its literal time is the past, for its central character is Mary of Nazareth; and as the title indicates, it is another family play. And it is definitely in the contemporary key in the manner in which it presents the interplay of family and neighborhood: the rise of family fortunes under neighborhood approval, the fall of family prestige and consequent calamity to individual members of the family when community disapproval is intense. It shows the close alignment between social status and economic security; the indirect influence of political chicanery upon individual well-being; the power of military-dominated government; the drive of a racial minority to assert its rights—all so long ago that some seeing the play are tempted to exclaim, "This is yesterday reprimanding today with more authority than today can speak to itself." Others see in the play only, or chiefly, a moving human story, built with respect and simplicity out of the imagination of the play-wrights, who have attempted to give us a picture of what Mary's other children, her grandchildren, her in-laws, and her neighbors may have been like, going about their daily tasks, meeting life and love and death like the rest of us, and speaking a language as natural on the stage as that which we speak in our own daily routines today. If these characterizations are apocryphal, they seem none the less real as the story moves along. The main story moves, of course, even more than is the case in *Abe Lincoln in Illinois*, in the minds of the audience. The Cowens take it for granted that they need not retell it; they make no attempt to enact the great scenes in Jesus' life; he never comes upon the stage. Instead, they do exactly what the title implies—they give us the portrait of a family as the daily lives, fortunes, destinies, of the family are affected by the rising and falling popularity of this one son who holds the public eye—and at times the public heart.

The family are rather a grumbling lot, in good healthy family fashion, on the morning when we first see them having breakfast together in the court-

109

yard. The night previous, Jesus has gone off on an extended teaching trip; and his brothers Joseph and Simon, eager young business men with financial responsibility for their own young families, are irritated that they have lost the best carpenter in Nazareth just at a time when they have a large barn to roof for one of the community's leading citizens. Moreover James, next after Jesus among Mary's sons, as a rising young rabbi feels that his prestige is threatened; his friends "are some of the most important men in town"; he doesn't relish the idea of a freak teacher for a brother. Judah, the youngest, has no time to be worried about his favorite brother's comings and goings because he himself is in love. The girl is Miriam, daughter of a leading household, and he has been allowed to see her *alone*, which means that her father approves the suit. Mary shares Judah's joy just as she shares everyone's happiness; no sense of duty about it; nothing especially "motherly" in any customary sense. She merely enters into other people's points of view and absolutely knows how it is with Judah. The aunt, Mary Cleophas, also joins the family breakfast, and her shrewd, humorous comments gently wet-blanket the complaints of righteous James. One feels that she has been a tower of strength to the family ever since

110

Mary was left a widow—a tower which is comfortably upholstered for leaning against. Not that Mary herself leans; Mary stands straight and strong through the hurrying days. One compromise she makes with petulant James and his somewhat harassed brothers: if Jesus does not return "within a reasonable length of time," some of the family will go to get him back. We realize when she promises that she will keep her word if necessary but that she really expects the commotion to blow over.

However, when the months go by and Jesus does not return, Mary is forced to carry out her promise. She goes with the other sons to Capernaum to persuade Jesus to come home; or perhaps she goes with the other sons to curtail the manner of their persuasion. Plainly she is reluctant, for she has that simple and dignified gift of letting people—even her own children—mind their own affairs. Indeed, the more we see of Mary's essential regard for the integrity of those whom her life touches, the more we understand how it is that her eldest son happens to make respect for human personality a major emphasis in his teaching. When Mary, James, Simon, and Joseph arrive at Capernaum, they stop at the wineshop of Selima, where the sons leave Mary while they go in search of their brother. She sits quietly

111

at a table and listens to the talk in the shop. At some
time we have all been in her situation—sitting unob-
trusively, asking an offhand question, hoping to
hear what people think of someone whose success is
public conversation and who matters very much to
us. Mary hears Selima bragging about the number
of Jesus' followers, about the business which comes
to her tavern just because he is teaching in the vicin-
ity. Mary also listens to what the travelers say as
they come and go, and as she listens she cannot refrain from asking a question or two of the serious and
rather charming young man across the table.

MARY: And they all believe in him. They all think he's
wonderful?

YOUNG MAN (*with glowing faith*): For *me*—he's the beginning
and the end.

MARY: Oh, I didn't mean *I* had any doubts about his being
wonderful. I only meant—did the *people* think so—

YOUNG MAN: I can only speak for myself. I would *die* for
him.

Then he tells her a bit about Jesus' teaching, about
his way of handling the tired but insistent crowds.
Spontaneously Mary says that she quite understands;
she knows his way with people. And when the young
man naturally asks if she too knows Jesus, she answers simply, "I know him very well. You see—he's
my son."

All the talk of him, the evidence of public esteem, naturally makes her still more eager to see her son again. We sense continually throughout the play that theirs has been a rare sort of companionship, that his being the eldest son who stepped into his father's place as head of the household when his father died has brought them sympathetically close together. She knows that he will come hurrying to her as soon as he hears that she is here. But instead, the brothers come back to report that he paid no attention to them when they sent him the message, "Your mother and brothers are here and want to see you." The message he sent back was simply, "*Who* is my mother—and *who* are my brothers?" Mary is incredulous. She finally draws forth the rest of his remarks; to the people on the hillside he had said, "*You* are my mother and *you* are my brothers!" Now Mary understands: he has merely used their message as a lesson; that's the way he teaches. They have never understood how he feels about people, she says—about common people, about all people. They should have heard the talk in this very wineshop. They should have heard what this young man beside her said—that he'd *die* for him! And she turns to introduce them to the young disciple.

113

I'd like you to meet my sons—(*She pauses, then realizes she can't make the introduction and adds.*) Oh, I'm sorry—I'm afraid I don't know your name—

YOUNG MAN: Judas. Judas Iscariot.

The curtain begins to descend slowly as MARY *introduces her sons, her hand confidingly on* JUDAS' *arm.* . . . .

There are excited preparations for Jesus' return to Nazareth when he has been invited—by the local rabbis themselves—to preach in the synagogue. Mary is roasting a lamb and baking bread; the daughters are preparing vegetables, furbishing the house; the neighbors, including some who have never paid much attention to the family before, are lending their best dishes and stopping to talk. Joseph and Simon, excited at the prospect, are planning to shine in reflected glory, perhaps to say a few words themselves in the synagogue if asked; and it is these brothers who, after Mary has gone into the house, open the gate to a Roman official. . . . . Whatever shadow of destiny hangs over *Family Portrait* is not made known in the ancient manner by oracles or augurs but by the simple incidents in daily life which sometimes, anywhere, seem to have a way of foreshadowing destiny. Thus in the case of this Roman. He has come to discuss terms of a contract for building Roman crosses. Plain wooden crosses, the sort upon which criminals are hung. Simon and Joseph

114

are keen to arrange the deal; there is money in it.
But James breaks in in time to forbid any dealings
with the Roman. "We don't do business with a for-
eigner." The Roman goes off angrily, and the sons
call in Mary to settle their squabble. She comes,
bringing the bread she is kneading out to the table
under the tree. She listens to the whole tale. Her
decision is quick and final. It springs from her nature
and not from any reasoned argument. There will be
no making of crosses.

I'm not blaming you for trying to get ahead—it's your
nature to be like that. But I don't believe in killing people—
no matter what they've done.

JOSEPH: Only the lowest sort of criminals—

MARY: Even so. What have we to do with a business like
that? And today—of all days! Jesus coming home—

A peddler arrives with gorgeous scarves, shawls,
and dress-lengths. Mary buys a new shawl, happily,
recklessly; a blue one. The excitement grows louder
in the street. Young Daniel, Mary's grandson,
rushes into the courtyard shrieking, "He's here! He's
here!"

MARY *goes to the open gate—stands for one moment, looking. Then
her arms fly out as she almost runs out into the road. The curtain starts
down. . . . .*

After Jesus has come—and gone—the family
courtyard is a very different place. Jesus has made

115

his speech in the synagogue—and he has been driven out. Mary tries to explain to her sister-in-law, or perhaps to herself, speaking reluctantly.

People weren't in the right frame of mind for him to come back just now. No one here had any real faith in him. But their local pride was stirred up. Then when he came—and you know how simple he is—and he went around without making himself important—just living here as he always did—well, they just couldn't accept him—that's all.

While the hush of disappointment is still fresh upon them and their most reasonable explanations do not quite reassure even themselves, Mendel, the marriage-broker who has arranged the betrothal of Judah and Miriam, comes to call. With him is the rabbi. Mary is glad to see them; Judah's happiness means much to her. But today the errand of the rabbi and Mendel is not pleasant. They state their business shortly: Aaron has called off the marriage between Judah and Miriam.

MARY: But *why?*

MENDEL: I hate to say this, Mary—and the words are my client's—not mine.

MARY: Go on.

MENDEL (*reluctantly*): Your family is getting a bad reputation. (*A long pause.*)

RABBI (*gently*): Because of Jesus.

Mary protests the unfairness of making Judah suffer for the actions of his brother, whereupon Mendel

116

reminds her that "things like this run in families. You can't tell where they'll break out next." Still, there is one thing Mary might do to make Aaron change his mind; Aaron has stipulated that if the marriage is to be consummated, Mary must never receive Jesus in her house again. She protests, indignantly; and at last the rabbi, exclaiming that he had come as a friend, speaks sharply. We see Mary walk over to the gate, open it, and stand there. Then she speaks "almost in a whisper."

I don't like to ask a rabbi to leave my house—but I can't have you talking like that about my son. The streets are free— you can say what you like in them. But this is his home.

The two men start for the gate; but the rabbi pauses, plainly moved.

I'm sorry, Mary. I lost my temper. (*Pause.*) All I know is— if he were my son—I'd be worried.

Deeply concerned by the rabbi's words, Mary is pacing the courtyard when young Judah comes bursting in. He is off to see Miriam; is almost out the gate before his mother can halt him. No time to break the news gently; she must speak at once. For a moment Judah cannot take in her words; they make no sense. Then with youth's quick perception of defeat at the hands of authority, Judah begs his mother to do what Aaron has asked. Disown Jesus,

117

cut him off—it is Jesus who is taking exception to
the accepted way of life, not Judah. When Mary
insists firmly, sadly, that this is Jesus' home too and
always shall be, Judah breaks away from her.

The gate closes sharply behind him. MARY *stands alone on the stage;
then with a gesture of complete and utter defeat, she crosses with leaden
feet to the table, sinks down on the bench and lays her head on her arms
and weeps brokenly.*

After all, both sons are hers. She holds both their
futures in her hands; and her hands are helpless.

Because the audience knows the story, the portent
of tragedy seems to hang over the dark streets of
Jerusalem on the evening when Mary and Mary
Cleophas come to the city to hunt for Jesus. There
has been talk that he is in danger. Only a week ago
the people were acclaiming him a hero; perhaps
their enthusiasm was too audacious, for now the authorities are irate and the soldiers are said to be
gathering. Mary wants to find her son—now—and
to see with her own eyes how things are. A man
comes hurrying by, and they stop him to ask directions. Happily Mary recognizes Judas Iscariot, but
Judas is short spoken and evasive tonight. He tells
them where Jesus is staying; in fact, he has just left
the place, but he has no time to show them the way.
With gathering apprehension the weary women push

on to the designated house of Nathan the water-
seller. But they are too late. Everyone has gone.
In an upper room the table stands still covered with
dishes, candles still burning. It is a setting the audience knows well; Da Vinci's "The Last Supper," but
without the figures. Jesus' cloak is still on a chair.
His mother picks it up anxiously. The night will be
cold; he is always forgetting to take care of himself.
Yet there is no use to go out hunting for him; he
will have to come back to this room. It is typical of
Mary that she does not rant or dash about. She has
the elemental, uncluttered simplicity of a country
woman who makes forthright acceptance of things
as they come, good and bad. Another guest of the
house comes in, a lovely young woman with a kind
of quiet radiance about her. Her name is Magdalen.
She talks with Mary, seeming to sense how hungry
the woman is for first-hand news of her son. Certainly Mary could have found no one who understands him more loyally. Magdalen owes him so
much; hers is the intense loyalty one has for a teacher
who has freed the spirit.

Sudden noise in some distant street. The shouting
grows nearer, angrier; the women are rigid with
fear; the reassuring words of Magdalen are muffled
by thick dread. Suddenly Mary rushes to the win-

dow, flings it open; but Nathan thrusts her aside. "Get away from that window! They've arrested him! I don't want my house mixed up in this!" Mary is stunned. She cannot understand that this is happening to her son—but even as the unreality sweeps over her, she knows that it is true. She is acting automatically now, taking up the cloak he has left behind. He will need this cloak; they may keep him all night.

The shouts in the street reach a crescendo and MARY *stands,* JESUS' *cloak clasped in her arms as she hears the words—"Crucify him! Crucify him!"*

The play could stop at this point and be registered as tragedy in the minds of the audience, for there is the stamp of finality upon the figure of Mary, the stamp of defeat upon her son. But of course life has to go on for Mary and for her family; and the story goes on in the minds of the audience. We pick up the stage story some years later on a late afternoon in midsummer. Excitement again in the courtyard of Mary's home. This is the day of the betrothal of her beautiful young granddaughter, Esther. The girl's fiancé and his father, Leban, are coming from Damascus. A radiant joy pervades everything, and Mary reminisces as she puts the finishing touches to things.

120

You'll be head of your own house—no old mother-in-law to make life miserable, the way I do around here. (*She smiles at Esther who smiles back a bit shakily.*) And then, before you know it, your babies will be coming along. Wait till you have your first one! Nothing makes you feel so important as your first baby. I'll never forget mine. . . . . (*She breaks off—a shadow crossing her face.*) Look—there's the first star! Like the one at Bethlehem—(*Pause. Throws off mood with effort.*) There now, don't let me start talking about—about when I was young— or the company won't get any supper!

Only that brief reaching back to an earlier day— it may have been largely a matter of inflection, but these few words gave Judith Anderson the opportunity to achieve one of the high points of her interpretation.

As if the betrothal were not excitement enough, Judah's wife, Deborah, is about to have her first baby, and Judah comes hurrying in with the midwife. Old Mendel the marriage-broker arrives, bragging happily of Leban and his son. Mary interrupts the chatter to ask a grave question: When Mendel first met Leban and his son in Damascus last year, did he tell them about her family? Yes, Mendel insists. But is he sure he told them about everyone, left no one out? Before the question is answered, Leban and his son are there. Presentations; a few final words about dowry arrangements; the young people meet and are plainly delighted. But still Mary's unanswered question. She turns to Leban.

> I'm sorry to interfere at the last minute like this—but since no one else will speak, I'm afraid I'll have to. I can't let this go on without saying something. . . . . My oldest son—he got into some difficulty with the authorities.
>
> LEBAN (*hesitantly, to Mendel*): Is that James—the one who's away?
>
> MARY: No, not James. The one I mean is dead. (*Pause.*) He was killed.
>
> LEBAN: Oh, I'm sorry. An accident?
>
> MARY: They thought he was trying to stir up trouble and they—they crucified him.
>
> LEBAN: *Crucified* him!
>
> MARY (*with sudden desperation*): Don't you understand? Don't you see what I'm trying to tell you? My son was Jesus of Nazareth! (*Her voice breaks and she makes a gesture of helplessness and turns away.*) Now you know!

Everyone begs Leban not to let this make a difference; it was a long time ago. Suddenly Mary Cleophas realizes the true reason for Leban's embarrassment.

> Save your breath! The man's never heard of him!
> (*The others stare at* LEBAN *with incredulity. He mumbles in his embarrassment.*)
>
> LEBAN: Well—you see—I'm afraid—I—I—I live so far away—

The brothers begin proudly to tell of Jesus' works, of the fact that even yet some people are keeping on

122

with his work. Leban would like to know what it was he taught. So Mary tells him the simple things she remembers: about loving your enemies and living with a purpose; about not being "afraid of people who kill the body; because, after that, there is nothing more they can do"; about always remembering "that human life is beautiful—and noble—because it houses God." Leban asks if anyone has ever tried it, "to live the way he taught?" It would be interesting, he thinks, to see what would happen if anyone did try. "It's too simple!" says Mary Cleophas. And Mary herself thinks this may be so.

> You know, I think that's what caused all the trouble. They couldn't understand that it was all just as simple as that. That there wasn't something behind it.

The entrance of the rabbi cuts short the talk. The family goes into the house to drink the betrothal wine. Only Mary lingers to speak with Judah, who is coming down the stairs from his room. Things are going a little slow with the confinement, he tells her.

MARY (*with careful casualness*): If the baby's a boy—what are you going to name him?
JUDAH: We haven't decided.
MARY: I wish—
JUDAH: What, Mother?
MARY: Will you do something for me, Judah?
JUDAH: Of course I will! What is it?

Voices from above interrupt, and Judah starts for the stairs, Mary following him.

> If it's a boy, will you name him for your brother—(*Hesitantly.*) After Jesus, I mean?
>
> JUDAH: Why—why, yes, Mother. I'll talk to Deborah about it—(*He leans over the railing of the staircase and kisses her.*)
>
> MARY: It's a nice name. (*As* JUDAH *starts to run up the stairs, she adds:*) I'd like him not to be forgotten.

"I'd like him not to be forgotten." The indeterminate ending; the uncertainty going on. The conclusion of the play, the final ending, is in the minds of the audience just as the high points of the story have been in the minds of the audience. Perhaps no two persons find the same story or the same ending. *Will* Mary's son be forgotten? Indeed, some ask, has he ever been remembered? Because the audience is so much a part of the ongoing story, the play has a time dimension which gives it something of the magnitude of tragedy: man looming large against the centuries. But none of the finality of tragedy, only the threat of it, the threat of ultimate defeat. As the story stands—upon the stage of a theater or upon the stage of history—"the stone is rolled away." The door is open.

If at the moment a good many American playwrights seem somewhat preoccupied with studying the prevailing social confusions as focused under the microscope of family life or examined through the telescope of the past, other playwrights approach their subjects by particularizing a more general phase of life today. Katharine Dayton and George S. Kaufman satirize Washington life in *First Lady* for the benefit not only of those who know their politics and protocol first hand but also for the columnists' clientele who know their Washington more intimately if rather less accurately. A play as amusing as *Having Wonderful Time* affords Arthur Kober a chance to show the holiday opportunities as well as the starved lives of "white-collar" citizens who fight for a measure of leisure and then do not know exactly what to do with the leisure when they get it. A more fanciful theater-piece gives Victor Wolfson a means of saying much the same thing in *Excursion*, wherein on the stage the fantasy reached toward reality through Whitford Kane's believable portrait of the naïve and hearty Captain Obadiah. In *Ladies and Gentlemen* Charles MacArthur and Ben Hecht fashion for Helen Hayes and Philip Merivale a piece which looks at several types of American citizen who may be subject to jury call—at the young Hollywood studio secretary who has "not spoken to a man without a notebook in her hand in

125

the last six years"; at the bus-driver's wife who, ardently believing in prenatal influence, spends much of her jury time considering a picture of Joe DiMaggio; at the script-writer; the Yale man; the undertaker; the barber. Although this new vehicle for Mr. MacArthur's wife came by way of the Hungarian of Ladislaus Bus-Fekete, it is definitely the contemporary United States (West Coast) as it crosses the lights to us, however it may vacillate between the mood of facile, brittle wisecracking and the mood of romantic sentiment, the latter mood affording Miss Hayes and Mr. Merivale an opportunity, in the moonlight, to discover how much at-one they are on important things in life like the music of Puccini, the stories of Conrad, and the satisfactions of minute steak. The press department dodges this mood mixture by calling the play "a murder-trial comedy-drama"; audiences seem to accept it as comedy of our own times, their critical faculties pleasantly swept aside by Miss Hayes's personality, as audiences some years ago were swept along by Mrs. Fiske's pacing of a not entirely dissimilar play, *Ladies of the Jury.*

Going back to a New Hampshire village in times which many of us can still remember, Thornton Wilder is able to give us a salty parable of life in

Our Town, which is meant to be the place where all of us are born, live, love, die. This play, made the more real by Frank Craven's impersonation of the Stage Manager (and by Wilder's own acting when Craven was out of the cast), tells of two individual families and the larger family of the community within a framework of homespun ideals which almost all Americans like to have repeated to them. Through the Stage Manager the playwright philosophizes about an American way of life too gentle to be epic, too sad to be tragic, but with a note too genuine to be forgotten. On a note more keyed to the tempo of the immediate day Philip Barry in *The Philadelphia Story* takes a satirical fling at aspects of a particular publishing trend, and Samuel Raphaelson in *Skylark* uses the hectic demands of the advertising game as the springboard of a sprightly story. Indeed, both these latter plays, coming forth in the same season, treat theme and characters in the same sprightly manner which marks the comedy of manners.

The Philadelphia Story is about Tracy Lord, young daughter of the aristocracy of American wealth, who has divorced one husband and is about to take a second when the curtain goes up. Her father (who hasn't been behaving so well lately; there's an actress

127

in his life) thinks that Tracy is minus "an understanding heart," and her recent husband considers
her "a virgin goddess" who has always had so many
of the luxuries of cushioned existence that she's never
even tried to adapt herself anywhere along the line.
But it is what a young writer on the staff of the magazine *Destiny* thinks of Tracy that brings about the
big situation of the play, just as it is the Lords' fear
of *Destiny*'s publisher, Mr. Sidney Kidd, that brings
the young chap into the Lord household on the eve
of Tracy's second matrimonial step. The Lords are
afraid that Kidd will publicize the father's playtime
activities with the actress, and so they lure the publisher off with promise of an exclusive story about
the Lords' home life and Tracy's swank wedding.
Which brings the writer onto the scene along with
a lady photographer. And the writer finds himself
attracted to Tracy, maybe somewhat in love with
her. They drink champagne together—and all at
once Tracy thinks this would be a swell night for a
swim. So they swim, the two of them, just like children, in the altogether. And somehow or other—
the result is more persuasive in the theater than in
any reporting of the metamorphosis—next morning
Tracy is a different girl. She sees that she was on
the brink of marrying a stuffed shirt; she realizes

that her first husband is really all right. And the young writer? Well, he's glad to have been of such service. Naturally there is a little more to the story than this; the Lords develop, but don't quite finish, a scheme to blackmail Kidd the publisher, whose magazines include *Dime* and *Spy* as well as *Destiny;* and through dialogue and situation Barry thrusts a good deal of satire at a type of magazine using what is referred to irreverently as "snide, corkscrew English." The staff member illustrates by improvising a paragraph about the boss as *Dime* might print it:

.... No lightweight is balding, beetlebrowed Sidney Kidd, no mean displacement his. None before him but writer Wolfgang Goethe has known all about all. Gigantic was Goethe's output, bigger still is Kidd's.

This play is Barry in *Holiday* mood once more; and audiences have welcomed his return to the familiar milieu, as they have welcomed Katharine Hepburn, for whom he is said to have patterned his Tracy Lord.

In *Skylark* Lydia Kenyon is on the brink of divorce instead of second marriage. She is the neglected wife of an unfaithful husband—because Tony Kenyon has been "sleeping with his business," an advertising agency for which he neglects her. After eleven years of this, Lydia is pretty tired of it. So when a poetic and mellowly inebriated lawyer

129

friend who likes to look beyond mundane success huskily propounds his philosophy of romantic freedom, Lydia listens. And then goes into action. Her course of action first astounds, then distresses, and finally wakes up her successful young advertising man; and though the play veers sharply after the first act, the proceedings are diverting fare for an audience, with Gertrude Lawrence racing to comedy's happy ending and Donald Cook catching up with her for the final curtain, Glenn Anders as the young lawyer having strolled his lugubrious poetic way out of the picture. Not a vital commentary on our times, yet as contemporary as the women's hats or the men's slack suits of its season, with a theme sufficiently pertinent to make husbands in an audience conscious of their wives' side glances as Tony Kenyon's absorption in his job is dramatized before them.

Clifford Odets met the expectations of his admirers a bit less with *Rocket to the Moon*, produced the same season as the Barry and Raphaelson plays. It has snapshot recognizability in figures like Ben Stark, D.D.S., and his father-in-law, Mr. Prince; there is reality in the picture given of Stark and the girl Cleo as they are caught in a pocket of life so common that it is poignant; there is remarkable verisimilitude in the easy vernacular of the Odets dialogue. Perhaps, indeed, *Rocket to the Moon* is too realistically ordinary; it is hard for many to grow concerned about these people as we are concerned about the characters of *Awake and Sing*, which seems to transmute realism into something meaningful. Morris Carnovsky's Jacob and Luther Adler's Moe Axelrod in the earlier play were full remarkable portraits, while Carnovsky's Dr. Stark and Adler's Mr. Prince in the newer play stay with us chiefly as neatly faithful duplicates of people we've seen almost anywhere and may forget any time. These are the types Odets chose to draw; and of course the playwright should not be reprimanded too much for his choice of material any more than an audience for its reaction. The play centers around Ben Stark. He is a humdrum fellow, one of the millions, "as mixed up as the twentieth century." He is married not congenially; "drip, drip, the matrimonial waters go, and a man wears away." Love through the person of his office girl touches him, lightly, transiently; and passes on. But something—something rather vague—is left to Stark. He tries to put it into words for Mr. Prince.

. . . . For years I sat here, taking things for granted, my wife, everything. Then just for an hour my life was in a spot-

131

light. . . . . I saw myself clearly, realized who and what I was. Isn't that a beginning? Isn't it?

A beginning of what? Stark doesn't know, any more than the rest of us are likely to understand when we have such feelings. "Sonofagun! . . . . What I don't know would fill a book!" he admits as he turns out the last light, closes the office door behind him, and so brings down the curtain on one more play with an indeterminate ending. Indeterminate if there *is* a beginning afterward for Ben Stark, D.D.S. Odets has given us the picture and wishes to let it rest there. Like most of our playwrights (fortunately, more often than not) he does not offer a complete solution to any contemporary question he may have raised. If there is a full answer, he leaves it to Stark and us.

In an age of questioning, anyone may offer an answer. Patient audiences seem never too jaded for one more hope. But then most audiences—which means most of us most of the time—are not primarily looking for a solution to our problems when we go to the theater. Certainly we are not consciously anticipating additional stores of wisdom. Now and then we get them—both wisdom and solution—and we know in our more perceiving moments that the passing-on of such a "lift" is the prime function of the theater; but most of us actually go to the theater from a simple, a fundamental impulse: we go to the theater because we love a good story. We like to see our fellow-humans winding their mysterious way through the labyrinths of motivation—the longings, desires, passions, hopes, which furnish the suspense for our own tomorrows. And the playwrights write their plays for a similar fundamental reason: they like to tell a story. If their story happens to have a "thesis" which bespeaks some current conviction, or happens to have a setting which reflects some current scene, or happens to utilize in dialogue today's idiosyncratic patter—then it merely happens so. At least it merely happens so with all but a small minority of writers for the stage. The story is the playwright's real reason for being—a story told in his own way, because he is the sort of person he is. If he wavers from expressing himself as he is—which is to say from interpreting life as he sees it with characters he knows in a situation he understands—then he baffles both himself and his audience. That is, if his play ever gets into production.

It is with such a playwright at the very crisis of his wavering that S. N. Behrman deals in his comedy which bears the ironic title, *No Time for Comedy*. For some years Behrman has displayed a gift for stage

133

talk barbed with wit and tinctured with thought, urbanely delivered by characters who are, in the easy argot of the very kind of persons he writes about, "civilized." Given a man and a woman and another man—or another woman, or both—plus a suave setting wherein to veer toward a tangle which they can sidestep, and he has been able to make an evening in the theater a rather sparkling affair for us. He has generally done this deftly and honestly; and has, as it were, succeeded in juggling his dramatic situation in one hand while he juggled ideologies of the day in the other, using the modulated voices of his characters to broadcast his own curiosities, as from a loud-speaker turned properly low in a drawing-room (or a studio, or a terrace) where ideas as well as thin sandwiches are served up along with the cocktails. With quips and cracks and even longish thoughtful speeches he has touched investigatingly socialism, capitalism, fascism, and other isms of the times while keeping us smiling, now and then laughing, at the actions of his characters, the incongruities of their opinions against the reality of their daily "civilized" lives. He has appeared to find it fascinating—amusingly *and* painfully fascinating—to steer a course through the uncharted confusions of these times, until indeed his *Wine of Choice* seemed perilously near being lost in a fog of confusions, with the "radicals" and the "liberals" on board sending up rockets which only added to the confusion of many of us who were safely (but not too happily) ashore in our orchestra seats. Was Behrman getting, to paraphrase one of his own lines, "profound or merely obscure"? Was he groping to say something that he didn't, or couldn't, say any too clearly? Was he becoming somehow a bit self-conscious, in the wrong way? Or was he feeling the worst of all sensations for the creative writer, "written out"? He seems to have given us an answer in *No Time for Comedy*. At least he has admittedly dramatized what might be called the autobiography of his conflicting creative impulses during the immediate past.

For *No Time for Comedy* is about the playwright Gaylord Esterbrook and his "dilemma." The dilemma is whether to go on writing bright comedies in a world that's full of troubles. The story is of Gay Esterbrook and his wife and the other woman. The wife is a brilliant actress known on the stage as Linda Paige; and she is wise and gallant, i.e., she knows her husband and finds a way to meet his imminent defalcation from hearth and art. The other woman? She is "a Lorelei with an intellectual patter," as Philo Smith, her banker-husband, desig-

135

nates her; and she would have Gay turn from comedies to something of deep social significance. Philo,
reticent and unhappy, thinks that he sees pretty well
through this young lady builder-upper who is his
wife. He knows that Amanda has set herself the
job of being an Influence to other men; it doesn't
matter to her that they are really without true talent.
Linda retorts with a bit of asperity when he warns
her that the same thing is happening to Gay.

My husband is not mediocre, Mr. Smith. My husband is
brilliant.

PHILO: Then she will persuade him that he is profound.

As Amanda almost does. She has already persuaded
Gay to begin a meaningful drama of the war in
Spain; if there is no part in such a drama for his
wife . . . . well, he owes more to "the world" than
to Linda. Such is the situation which is set up; the
rest of the play is the battle of Linda to save her husband *and* the playwright. The result is amusing action, swift dialogue, and smartly plausible characters
as interpreted by actors like Katharine Cornell,
Margalo Gillmore, Laurence Olivier, Francis Leder-
er, and John Williams. Listening to them—or reading the printed lines—we have a feeling that we
are listening in on some of the doubts which must
have been assailing Behrman himself, with Gay

Esterbrook of the play voicing the questionings and
Linda the reassurances, the reaffirmations. Thus in
the first act, when the two first skirt the issue, the
effect—without, one hopes, drawing the parallel too
close—is like the debates we sometimes hold with
ourselves.

GAY: What the hell's the use of kidding myself—I've got
nothing to say.

LINDA: But you say it charmingly!

GAY: The hell with that. I'm sick of that. It's no time for
that.

LINDA: Never was such a time. The world's depressed. This
is the moment to be gay, if possible.

GAY: That's like calling for a minuet in a plague town.

LINDA: Why not?

GAY: You live in an aura of exhibitionism or you couldn't
ask me a thing like that. Look around you. Pick up a newspaper. Look at the world. And you expect me to go on bab-
bling lightly in a never-never land.

LINDA: You underestimate yourself. Your plays are gay,
they're gallant and witty. Occasionally they're touching. What
more do you want? Do another—for God's sake—and for
mine. . . . .

When we come to the third act, we find Linda
speaking out very clearly in her final fight to save
Gay's integrity to do the thing he can do.

. . . . I beg of you, Gay, don't throw away your charming
gift, don't despise it. . . . . Is it more profound to write of death
of which we know nothing than of life of which we may learn

137

something, which we can illuminate, if only briefly, with gaiety, with understanding? Gay, I beg of you, don't turn your back on the gift you have, the instinct you have, the power you have. . . . .

And when, shortly before the curtain is to come down, Gay admits that he is unsure of this new play he has been writing; in fact, is sure that it is "inadequate to its idea," that it is only "indignation without form—passion without authority—not tragic, but thin, petulant," Linda speaks out plainly what we suspect must have been the growing convictions of Behrman himself.

But even if it were everything you wanted it to be I still shouldn't be impressed. I am not impressed by the dead. Your hero says to the girl that in Spain he learned how to die and now he will practice what he has learned. . . . . That does not impress me—that he knows how to die. Millions of people know how to die—Stoics and fanatics—the insensitive and the robots. In any case it is an art that sooner or later Nature imposes on all of us. No, the difficult thing, the admirable thing is to live. That requires ingenuity, that requires skill, that requires imagination—that is the index of civilization—the ability to live, not the ability to die. Don't spin for me fantasias of death. Imagine for me variations of life. . . . .

And this is what Behrman has done. He has staged some "variations of life" for us, thus achieving what Gay Esterbrook hopes to achieve when at the end of the play he finds the solution to his di-

138

lemma by dramatizing it—in a comedy. We see refracted through *No Time for Comedy*, as Gay hopes
audiences will see refracted through his play, "the
disturbances and the agony of the times." Today
refracted through comedy, because that is the Behrman way; through what the labeler would label,
with no doubt at all, comedy of manners.

But why label? Most of the time it is not so easy
as this; we seem able to classify plays today chiefly
by elimination. We may say blithely, in our best
ex cathedra accent, that any play is comedy when it
eventuates in indecision allowing too much hope of
ultimate adjustment for tragedy, or when it focuses
our interest upon the ultimate welfare of the characters instead of upon the intricacies of plot which
mark the melodrama and the farce. Classification
by elimination. And then the task begins of applying
our pronouncement to a particular play. Or, as
likely as not, someone comes along with an entirely
different slant on our self-satisfied dictum. Perhaps
—just perhaps—an understanding of the elements
of comedy might help a playwright—some playwrights—to more integrated structure. Perhaps—a
slender perhaps—some statement of rules, if they
could ever be agreed upon, might help some critics
and professors to help other critics and professors to

know what they meant when they labeled a play. Or perhaps—the thinnest perhaps of all—some audiences might sit more snugly in their seats if they knew for sure whether they were witnessing serious comedy or tragedy, sentimental comedy or melodrama, high comedy or farce.

But probably an easier reason for sorting labels is that to some persons analysis is fun. It is the creative process in reverse, and once in a while the wheels begin to mesh in the other direction so that the labeler finds himself setting up scenes and characters of his own. Not that it is necessarily nobler to set up scenes than to examine and appreciate them; for that matter, the iconoclasts have as much place in the civilized world as the innovators. Labels are merely a short cut for exchanging critical thought, a kind of shorthand for dramatic perception, a springboard for emphatic disagreements. So that when an individual says of a play, "*Here* is a comedy," he is characterizing himself quite as much as diagnosing the play. Someone else may see a closed door—tragedy, where *he* sees a wobbly lock which may at any minute give way and allow the door to swing open. Someone else may see hilarious horseplay—farce, where *he* sees a wistful figure preferring ridicule to pity. Someone else may see daring for daring's sake,

140

a life of excitement in which something must keep happening no matter to whom—melodrama, where *he* sees braggadocio cloaking unfulfilment. Each onlooker has a right to his own last word; each labeler a choice of the labels. Fortunately, however, there are some comedies so plainly born of the humor which is perspective that even the most punctilious will reach for the comedy label.

III.

MELODRAMA WITH A MEANING

WE ALL HAVE MOMENTS WHEN WE ARE UNABLE TO come forth with the expected answer to some question about the highlights of our novel-reading or theater-going, or about the big events of our own lives. These questions spring at us unawares—from some fellow-traveler, from a teacher or student, even from some reporter who is compiling another newspaper "symposium." We know the sort of thing we ought to say, but perversely we think of the wrong thing. We are asked about the great scenes we remember from the novels we have read, and we understand perfectly well that the questioner is thinking of Literature. Yet instantly *we* think of such scenes as Rudolph Rassendyll riding through the streets of Strelsau, with the girl in front of the inn shouting deliriously, "If he's red he's right!" while the real king is prisoned in a dungeon in the castle of Zenda. Not at all what the inquirer wants; not significant enough. Just a story. . . . . So he tries us on the high moments of our own lives—we might be expected to do better there; after all, no one knows so well as we what moments have been big. But do we do better? No, we are more than likely to recall the afternoon on a ship near the equator (as if that mattered!) when the second cook jumped overboard and a lifeboat was manned for rescue while the captain stood rigid on the bridge, his hand clutching a gun—to save the boy from sharks if need be. Not in the least what the questioner is looking for; this is not an event, it is merely an exciting incident. Just a thrill. . . . . But there is still our experience in the theater to fall back upon. And then, instead of neatly remembering the nuances of Forbes-Robertson's Hamlet as they differed from Gielgud's and Howard's and Evans', we find ourselves wanting to tell of that split second of dismay when the Girl of the Golden West was concealing the wounded hero in the loft and the drop of blood splashed down upon the hand of the sheriff. Not the true Art of the theater, this. Just melodrama. . . . .

Precisely. Story for story's sake; exciting incidents; thrills. And whenever, in the theater or while reading a book or listening to a raconteur, we find ourselves held tight to the story as such, breathlessly

143

watching the involvements of plot tangle and un-
tangle themselves, we can be sure that we are caught
in the spell of what the term-maker calls "melodrama." That is, we could be sure if we were able
to take time out from the story to analyze. If analysis does come, later, we may decide that it was
pleasure enough, and a legitimate pleasure, to be
gripped with the excitement of what-happens-next;
or we may feel that we were merely cheated into approval. Now Anthony Hope (or someone else,
Dostoievsky for instance) might have conceived a
strong psychological study of a man who is compelled to impersonate an imprisoned king. In this
study we might be held as tensely and ask as frequently, "What happens next?" but our interest
would obviously be differently centered; the focus
would be on character, and the involvements would
grow unerringly out of the characters. In so far as
the plot movements in this hypothetical character
study of another Rudolph Rassendyll were highly
tense and colorful, we might say that those particular
scenes were "melodramatic," and perhaps point out
in justification of the writer (and of ourselves) that
in life too we have the spectacular, as we have it
also in great tragedies like *Hamlet* and *Macbeth;* but
we would never call this psychological study as a

144

whole melodrama, as we are inclined to call *The Prisoner of Zenda* with its incidents piling up swiftly one after the other, all in an aura of romantic ideals, with no apology given or expected.

Just as the Anthony Hope romance conjecturally might have been different, it is also possible that if someone were to push us far enough concerning the incidents we remember out of our own lives he would manage to build for himself a story about the characters (or about us) which so depended upon sound psychologizing that the characters would transcend the incidents. One wonders, however, if he might not first find himself asking, "Did the sharks get the boy or was he saved?" before he asked, "Why did the boy jump overboard?" and begin inquiries into the environment-heredity factors which must have conditioned the second cook to the desperate state he was in as the ship crossed the equator that afternoon. Once he reconstructed his story from the psychological angle, however, the main interest would not be on the melodramatic. Whenever character motivation comes in to this extent, and the demand for plausibility exceeds the desire for the swift sweep of exciting action, the story ceases to be melodrama. Or at least such characterization and plausibility

145

were not included in the formula for melodrama when pasting labels was an easy gesture.

Melodrama for the old days and the old ways was a much more clear-cut proposition than it is today. Then it usually presented good people and bad people who changed little but moved around a great deal during the course of the play. The audience knew why the good were deserving of their final high estate and why the bad were deserving of their final gnashing of teeth: the good maintained the moral standards and the bad took liberties with the romantic ideals, which generally passed as ethical ideals. In a day when standards of sexual morality, even dual standards, dominated most of the other ethical concerns of society, it was comparatively easy to keep the heroine "pure" and the hero "high minded." Since the audience agreed upon the standards, they could turn their attention to following the involvements of plot without undue mental strain. Generally all that was needed for a sure-fire old-style melodrama was an impossible situation from which someone valiantly escaped in order to be caught in further dilemmas from which he likewise escaped—or was rescued—until both himself and the audience were spent with excitement, at which time he grabbed up his standard and waved it over the heads of a cheering crowd, all of whom would gladly have laid down their heads upon any make-believe block under any papier-mâché chopping-knife in order to save—well, what? Anyway, something important.

In those days a playwright could make a hero out of a deserving young man falsely accused; he could make villains out of three distinguished citizens—a banker, a general, a magistrate; and he could be sure that the audience would confine their questions to the involvements of plot: the conviction of the young man for a crime he never committed, his spectacular escape after twenty years, the noble and courageous retribution with which he marked the end of the three villains—curtain by curtain. But in these days even Edward Dantés would have to wait for a playwright to explain that the magistrate happened to be a grudge-holding individual because, say, of some childhood experience with the corner grocer who never forgave the little boys who soaped his windows on Halloween; he would have to pause while the general who coveted the hero's sweetheart was accounted for by an infancy starved of all feminine influence; he would have to wait until the banker who coveted the hero's ship was proved helpless before the influence of his grandfather's passion for collecting old pennies. In fact, everybody would have to be adequately motivated and then a few neat phrases added about the folly of being a general anyway and going to the best of wars, about the antisocial tendencies of the banking business as a whole, and about the political philosophy of any system of government which produces magistrates. The story after it was thus motivated and annotated to the satisfaction of the contemporary audience might still be a melodrama, but it would not have the fear, fury, and fireworks of the original stage version of *The Count of Monte Cristo*. The current social consciousness, if not conscience, has stayed the tempo of melodrama.

Or try to get a contemporary audience to sit on the edge of their seats in trepidation lest Pauline leave the lowborn dissembler who has tricked her into marriage and walk out on her parents who have participated in the deceit; try to get them to applaud the pure young girl's pure devotion which holds her fast to her lawful spouse. The present-day audience would be thinking of the good jobs she might get herself, or of the W.P.A. which might rescue her father. In fact, with the crumbling of the standards upon which *The Lady of Lyons* rested, the play becomes farce for our day or demands a re-writing

148

with contemporary character motivation. Today even in melodrama we reach for convincing characterization; we need to have our motivations clearly figured out and plausibly presented. The new criteria are more suitable for our frame of mind but somewhat hard on the playwright who would like to produce one more old-time thriller.

The present tendency toward realism of characters, adequately motivated, naturally brings melodrama nearer the edge of serious comedy or tragedy. Indeed, a story which in outline seems essentially melodramatic nevertheless sometimes shifts its emphasis so far to the side of character interest that the play itself will not be classed as melodrama at all. *Anna Christie*, for instance, has a melodramatic story: a shipwreck which brings a young stoker to a coal barge where he falls in love with a girl of questionable reputation and finally has to fight her hardened old father for her. Indeed, the theatricality of the "big scene" could be nothing but melodrama had O'Neill not taken such pains to motivate each character. He saw Anna as the sort of girl who would naturally break the news of her past life in just this sensational fashion because her background had no doubt contained a large measure of dime-novel, nickelodeon sentiment. But at no time does he allow

149

the action of the scene to overshadow the struggle of character. With desperation to be understood overcoming both her fear and anger, the girl is frantic to make plain to the men—and perhaps to herself—that her past life does not matter because she has never loved any man before. Her need to be believed in is far greater than her interest in the fight—greater than *our* interest in the fight. Action, however fast and furious, is second to character interest. The action may intensify our emotional response, but it never shifts the emphasis of the story away from inevitability through character, as is the case in, for example, *Outward Bound*, which in spite of the belief-in-character induced by Laurette Taylor, Florence Reed, Bramwell Fletcher, and others in the revival, is still a sort of contemporary morality play in a thrilling framework of melodrama.

Winterset, as we have seen, also presents a swift story in which improbabilities play a large part—so large a part that many persons will insist that the play can be only a new sort of melodrama. In real life it is not likely that Mio would find under one bridge the only witness who could clear his father's name, the man who framed his father, the judge who sentenced his father, and the innocent young girl with whom he himself falls in love. It seems even less likely, if one merely strings together the story elements, that the girl could suddenly persuade Mio that he has outgrown his revenge and then lead him to such transcendent heights of understanding that he does not even try to make his getaway but instead walks into the range of a machine gun which mows him down, and the girl with him. If the improbabilities of plot matter less to us than the boy's inner struggle with injustice, hatred, loyalty, love—then for us the play is tragedy. *If* we feel that Miriamne is adequately accounted for by her home and general environment, then her simplicity and naïveté have something of the quality of Cordelia's gentle honesty. But Miriamne is very near the "type" character of the older melodrama in which the innocent young thing was never really in danger because the noble purity of her character disarmed the most evil intention. For us Miriamne may seem to wear the raiments of realism chiefly because she lives in a tenement, belongs to a people who are discriminated against, and is the victim—through her brother—of very contemporary gang warfare. Perhaps the realism of setting and characterization is overpersuasive because we are watching the play against a backdrop of current social standards which we accept. Again the formula: standards, both romantic

151

and ethical, plus fast action and triumphant virtue. Therefore melodrama, contemporary style? Or tragedy, contemporary style? For the present there is no unanimity of opinion. We may have to wait for time to paste the final label on *Winterset;* time may season it into what everyone will readily recognize as melodrama characteristic of its period in American drama—a melodramatic story carrying a cargo of intended social significance.

The Little Foxes may come off no better among those who are interested in pigeonholing plays by types. Many are sure that this play, too, is melodrama. Surely Miss Hellman veers toward melodrama in her story: a conspiracy to cheat in an investment; stolen bonds which are the equivalent of the "papers" of the old-time thriller; the villain discovered, temporarily protected, exposed again through the sudden death of the man who had spared him only in order to override another antagonist; extortion versus jail; the last-curtain triumph of the innocent girl. Certainly there is in this curve of action the expected rise and fall of suspense, the entanglement of plot which melodrama has always fed upon. But in this play the characters are drawn, not merely sketched. Their motivations reach back into a former generation, and the outcome of the play seems to say something significant *in terms of character* not only for the generation portrayed but for our own day. True, the "good" characters remain good, and the "bad" characters are unredeemed to the end of the chapter; but the playwright gives us the feeling of increased stature in the husband whom we see, retrospectively, rising above the defeat of his marriage and the cheap chicanery of his brothers-in-law to serenity of judgment which makes him dare to withhold money from characterless relatives, whatever their sentimental claim upon him, and so to a dignified acquiescence to unseasonable death. We are also given the feeling that Alexandra not only moves from sheltered adolescence to young womanhood but proceeds from bewilderment to assurance and from dependence upon the old tangibilities to faith in the resources of her own personality. To many of us, these qualities in *The Little Foxes*, plus portraitures like those of Regina and Birdie which Tallulah Bankhead and Patricia Collinge are able to bring to full realization, cannot rise from the sort of play known for its frank absorption in the machinations of plot.

But notwithstanding today's insistence upon verisimilitude of character and commensurate motivation, some plays do hew to the line in the matter of

153

story for story's sake. For all the fact that they must carry a convincing load of psychological and sociological trappings, they still march at a brisk pace from the rise of the curtain to its final fall. Nothing long stays their single-minded purpose to excite, baffle, and thrillingly satisfy the audience. The Heywards' play, *Mamba's Daughters*, is an instance in kind. A glance at the ingredients of this theater piece would be enough to make a playwright envious who aspires to contrive a melodrama of the mellowest vintage. A trial for an opening scene; the conviction of the huge negress for beating up a white man who got her drunk and tried to cheat her; an old grandmother's interceding with the judge for the sake of her daughter's innocent baby; the judge's modification of sentence to five years at plantation labor on a near-by island, with provision that she shall never return to the mainland during that time; a hilariously irresponsible negro community who work themselves into fanatic religious fervor which precipitates a brawl; the razor-slashing of a ruffian whom nobody likes, his rescue by the huge negress who, violating her parole, makes a heroic attempt to save him by taking the dying man to the town hospital; her commitment to the penitentiary as punishment for breaking the parole; the

154

cherished little daughter's growing to lovely young womanhood and musical stardom, her betrayal by the ruffian whose life her mother had once saved; the mad night trip of the mother and the old grandmother across the marshes in the rain; the suffering of the girl, her success, her radio triumph; the ruffian's blackmailing of the girl through the mother and grandmother; the mother's final understanding of the blackmail and her second trip to the cabin in the marsh; the gun play; the murder; the mother's last note to her daughter; the suicide, alone, in the night. These are the story elements, and in this case the first glance gives the correct impression: *Mamba's Daughters* is unquestionably melodrama.

But since the play is melodrama for today, an outline of the action is by no means all the story as it comes across to us. There is something of race interpretation via the melodramatic. And the playwrights have tried to give characterizations that are larger, deeper, than the patently "type" sketchings of an earlier day. They make quite believable, at least during the performance of their drama before an audience, the almost savage loyalty of Hagar to her daughter Lissa, and old Mamba's practical, canny, common-sense standing up to life so that she wrests triumph from tribulation. As much a part

155

of the play as Lissa's fight with her seducer in the lonely cabin is her acceptance of disillusionment and disgrace as something to be lived through and used to enrich her art—melodramatic, of course, but with our own way of looking at things "realistically." Before the playwrights let the action of the main story get under way, they take care to give us a partial characterization of Hagar by means of the courtroom scene: Hagar charged with assault with intent to kill, accepting her five years' sentence to the penitentiary because she knows no way to explain herself; just a large, inarticulate negress whom we may take to be dangerous—until Mamba's explanations come forth. Then through what is told by old Mamba, Hagar's mother, the playwrights motivate Hagar's crime. She had taken "a washing" to a man on a boat alongside the wharf; he had given her "licker" to drink, which she had refused because she has a nursing baby, and then he had got out his guitar and started Hagar singing—singing, singing, until she was drunk with singing and the people on the wharf gathered round and she kept on singing, and drinking "licker" now until, as she reported to the judge, "I a little drunk wid de licker an' I very drunk wid de singin'." The fight, when the man tried to put out in his boat without paying for the washing, was an incidental affair to Hagar. He was "a puny little man" and she shook him—almost to death. That was all. This is Hagar—powerful, simple, the creature of her gift for song, and fanatically single-minded in her devotion to her child. In this opening scene also we begin to have drawn for us the lines of old Mamba's simple character—a type, no doubt, but individualized sufficiently for us to understand her canny swift thinking, the honesty of her declaration that she doesn't want things for herself "but fo' my daughtah an' my daughtah's daughtah."

As the story unfolds, it proceeds in seemingly leisurely fashion with nuances of deepened characterization. Against the background of the island store with the comings and goings of the plantation negroes, with their rivalries and jealousies, their threats, joys, and excitements, the character of the big inarticulate Hagar emerges into individuality. Out of her disorganized life and her amoral, primitive existence, a purpose begins to guide her—one not especially different from the purpose that led mothers to sacrifice in older melodramas, but now dramatized in terms of the struggle against habit and environment, both of which she can combat for the sake of giving her daughter Lissa a chance in an

157

indifferent contemporary world. Step by step, by making us understand Hagar the playwrights have made us ready to accept the sensational scenes which close their play. Knowing our melodrama, we know that something is going to happen when we see the "villain" back in the picture again, as swaggering and insolent as ever, only a scar on his cheek to remind anyone that Hagar has once saved his life. Knowing Hagar, we are prepared for the way things happen. Thus, having seen Gilly go off to the party with young Lissa's crowd, and also having been swept by the music into a further state of emotional expectancy, we are prepared for the return of one of Lissa's friends late in the night with news that Lissa has been given a drugged drink by Gilly and taken off in his car. We are prepared for Hagar's wild trip to Gilly's cabin, straight through the marsh, through rain and darkness. For speed and tension— and for good morality as well, with righteous anger avenging lost innocence—nothing in an older melodrama exceeds the scene in the cabin as Hagar strangles Gilly with her bare hands and Mamba arrives only in time to save his life and so keep Hagar, for Lissa's sake, from being branded a murderer. The old-style melodrama, however, would have had less room for the scene which follows this highly

theatrical climax, when Mamba counsels the vio-
lated Lissa with a philosophy around which playwrights of an earlier day would probably have made
a careful detour.

I knows, darlin'. I tries to bring yo' up to t'ink dat to hab
t'ings like this happen to yo' was the end ob eberyt'ing. I do
dat, Lissa, 'cause I neber want any unhappiness like dis to
come near yo'. But it come; an' I tells yo' de trut' now. Yo'
still got de same life, de same pretty face an' same pretty voice.
An' mighty soon now yo' goin' be in Noo Yo'k studyin' an'
learnin' an singin'—an' forgettin'.

Then comes Hagar's soothing word when Lissa is
feeling that all their work and all her own high
hopes are now in vain: Hagar will always take care
of Lissa, and the girl needn't worry.

If this cabin scene were less mechanically thrilling,
less sentimental, it might take on the aspect of a
play like *The Little Foxes*, with the portrayal of life
going on after temporary defeat. But both in situation and in the way Hagar's speech points forward
to a final act of devotion, it is far more akin to the
older type of melodrama, as is the promised final
sacrifice when it comes to fulfilment. Lissa has a
baby; it is born dead and is buried in the woods; no
one knows about it but Mamba and the old negress
Vina and Gilly. Lissa goes to New York and becomes a great success as a singer. Gilly threatens

159

Hagar that he will report the baby's death and ruin Lissa's future unless he gets money, a great deal of money. So Hagar and Mamba write to Lissa for money on pretext of needing it themselves. Finally the owner of the island store discovers what has been going on and explains to Hagar that she needn't have paid this money; Mamba was a regular midwife and there was nothing to hide in that infant's death if they had reported it to the authorities. Slowly now Hagar comprehends. This is her big night in more ways than one—it is the night of Lissa's radio debut, and it is the night when she must make her final sacrifice for Lissa. The daughter's voice is already coming in as the mother starts for Gilly's cabin. In the tradition of melodrama, we may expect exactly what follows: Hagar's attempt to keep Gilly from further extortion, his brazen plan to move to New York and do his blackmailing of Lissa direct, his gunplay to emphasize the threat, his miscalculation of Hagar's strength and swiftness. We expect the lamp to be crashed against the wall and the final struggle to be fought in the pool of light from the open doorway; we expect Hagar to kill him as she does. We expect, too, the powerful concluding action of the play, and would feel somehow cheated if we did not get it in Hagar's return to the store. The plantation negroes are still gathered there at the close of Lissa's broadcast. Hagar treats them all to candy balls from the large glass jar; she buys a whole "keg of bounce"; she's through with money. She announces that she's going away; no, not to Mamba in town; not to Lissa in New York; farther than that. If she's going that far, they must sing her a farewell. But not quite yet, says Hagar, she has some writing she wants to get down. So she dictates a crude statement that this night she has strangled Gilly Bluton "to deat'." The spellbound negroes will not believe her naïvely invented reason; anyway, they are all ready to swear that she hasn't been out of the store the whole evening. But Hagar sticks to her story and wants the note delivered to Proc Baggart in the morning.

. . . . Lis'en, eberybody. My ma say I ain't no good less she wid me to tell me what to do. Well, you go and tell um I do dis widout nobody tell me. I t'ink um out all by myself. I t'ink um like dis. (*She leans on counter and addresses them like a lawyer stating a case.*) Fifteen year ago dat Gilly Bluton daid. Dey say at de hospital five mo' minutes an' he ain't got a chance. Not a Gawd's t'ing between dat yaller nigger an' he Gawd 'cept only me. I gib um back he life. He life belong to me, enty?

Her friends agree; his life belongs to her. So, she says, she only took back what belonged to her. And

161

the cops don't need to ask any questions because she's written out all the answers, "an' dey got no call to ax nobody nuttin'." She'll hurry on her way. "Den now's de time fo' sing?" asks old Vina. Now is the time. Old Vina begins.

> We goin' to leabe yo' in de han',
> Sistuh Hagar, we goin' to leabe yo' in de han'. . . . .

But Hagar has taken up a revolver from the counter and stepped out the door into the darkness. There is a flash and a loud report. Voices call out. But deaf old Vina doesn't hear them and her back is toward the door. Obliviously she is singing on alone, finishing the stanza as the curtain comes down.

> Oh, my daughter,
> Goin' to leabe yo' in de han'
> Ob de kin' Sab-yor.

Thus the play ends on a note of finality which melodrama frequently shares with tragedy. To be sure, there is much of tragic stature about Ethel Waters' Hagar as she steps out the door, so much that we may feel that this character is fully drawn and meaningful; but the play is still melodrama, all the way, scene by scene. The standards it upholds are the old human standards and have comparatively little to do with the social concerns of the immediate present. Yet the play has indirect social implications for today. A submerged inarticulate race moves in on today, broadcasting its spirituals over a country-wide network to an enthusiastic audience of all races. Just a step from a Carolina plantation to New York. Lissa rises from the racial and economic obscurity which have been the customary lot of her people, to national fame; and her people follow her rise just as eagerly as they follow her songs. The songs come out of an earlier experience of a race of slaves, but Lissa's acceptance by the public—and her people's acceptance of her acceptance—is a present-day achievement. No one in the play says anything about "equal rights"; but there *are* radios in those little plantation stores, and music and money and justice move swiftly from the Charleston swamps to New York and back again. The simplicities of the plantation community stand out because they are shown against the larger and more complicated pattern of contemporary society. If considerable of our interest in the play as it moves before us, of our willingness to be swept into the spirit of the play, comes from the way in which the Heywards have written a melodrama with present-day interest in character, much of our attention also, through Miss Waters' portrayal, is drawn to a thoughtful interest in the background from which

163

the actors upon the stage have come to give interpretations of Hagar and Mamba and Lissa to Broad-
way.

It would be impossible to gauge how much of the
effectiveness of *Mamba's Daughters* comes from the
use of negro spirituals as integrating emotional background; indeed, even as we read the play, we seem
to hear the spirituals if we are caught into the spell
of the story. A similar background of songs—this
time the songs the doughboys sang in France—characterized Brock Pemberton's staging of Ransom
Rideout's prize-winning *Goin' Home* a decade earlier.
This too was an out-and-out melodrama and dealt
with barriers which a submerged race must face or,
less often, must make a social detour to avoid, as
the American negroes Israel and Jim tried to do.
With a tavern in a French seaport town for setting
and the days immediately following the signing of
the Versailles Treaty for period, Rideout contrives
his swift plot between the lift of a first curtain upon
soldiers ribaldly singing a refrain from "Mademoi-
selle from Armentières" and the fall of the final curtain as the soldiers, off for embarkation, are rousingly
telling the world "It's a Long, Long Trail." And
most of the other World War songs, proper or less
so, weave naturally through the story of Israel, the

New Orleans negro who married the French girl
Lise and took on much of the responsibility of the
inn along with matrimony. In the legitimate tradition of melodrama the second-act curtain crashes
down upon the scene of highest tension. Lise is no
better than she need be; and Major Powell, pretty
much intoxicated, has gone up to her room off the
balcony where she is awaiting him—the same major
who a bit earlier has happily discovered in Israel
the "best servant we ever had. . . . . He was a good
friend of mine, too. As much as one can be friends
with a nigger." While the major and Lise are upstairs, the mulatto Jim and other colored soldiers
are frolicking a bit with the big friendly Senegalese,
Samba Saar, who in bare feet and stripped to the
waist is doing a war dance for them, rhythmically
flashing his *coupe-coupe*. In the midst of this, Powell
appears on the balcony. The men below draw back
fearfully; Israel in a low tense voice wants to know
"what you all doin' in that room?" The intoxicated
Powell furiously gives them all one minute to clear
out; they clear—all except Israel, Jim, and Samba
Saar. Israel quietly warns Jim to get out also, and
Powell loudly threatens, "You better be movin', nigger!" And now we are ready for the "big curtain
scene" of melodrama.

165

TODAY IN AMERICAN DRAMA

JIM: Damn you, Major. I'm goin'. Yes, I'm agoin'. But it ain't you I'm going for! No, God damn you. I'm through with you and your damned army. I'm going to stay here in France. I'm gonna desert. Hear me? I'm gonna desert—to-night—see? God damn you and the States.
(*He exits as* MAJOR POWELL *lunges down the steps after him. Then* POWELL *sees* SAMBA.)

POWELL: Who's that nigger?

ISRAEL: Never mind him. You and me's got something to settle with each other.

POWELL: I haven't got anything to settle with a nigger.

ISRAEL: You got something to settle with a man.

POWELL: Why, you black dog! You're fixing for the damned-est thrashing a nigger ever got!

ISRAEL: You won't be the one to give it.

POWELL: Don't be too damned sure.

ISRAEL: There ain't anybody .... black or white .... that can lay up with another man's wife and get away with it.

POWELL: Wife! Why you liar .... she told me she wasn't your wife.

ISRAEL: So, you drunk fool—a negro's wife is plenty good enough for you! (POWELL *gets champagne glass, hurls it at* ISRAEL. *It misses mark.* SAMBA *rushes at* POWELL. *They fight.*) Leave him to me, Samba! Leave him to me! Samba! C'est mon affaire! Il est ivre! (SAMBA *throws* POWELL *on table. Then rushes to table up centre for coupe-coupe. Table is overturned.* SAMBA *starts toward* POWELL *with coupe-coupe.* POWELL *picks up chair to defend himself.*) No—not the knife, Samba! Look out, Mister Eddie—look out! (SAMBA *is about to stab* POWELL *when* ISRAEL *shoots* SAMBA. SAMBA *turns to* ISRAEL.)

SAMBA: Tu m'as tué—sale esclave!

166

And the curtain comes down as Samba drops dead. It lifts for the third act, as we are hoping it will, upon the scene only an instant later. Now Powell drags the body of Samba Saar into an adjoining room; Israel would help but is compelled to fall back in fear. The major soon gone, Israel, again left alone after a brief bitter encounter with Lise, has picked up the revolver and he is staring at the door behind which the body of Samba Saar lies when there is an insistent muffled rapping on the street door. He turns quickly. It is Jim outside the door; Israel hurries to open it, and Jim rushes in, terrified.

JIM: Hide me—hide me quick. They're after me.

ISRAEL: Sure I will! There's a place under the bar. But here—(*Israel gets a cognac bottle and glass from bar and offers* JIM *a drink.*) Drink this first—. Here—that'll steady you. Been deserting, eh? It's no fun desertin', Jim.

JIM: I'd 'a' got away only I was scared. Down there by the canal road I ran into two M.P.'s. Maybe if I hadn't run they wouldn't have noticed me. But I ran. I ran like hell. I—I felt like Joe must have felt with that mob after him. I dodged into a side street and gave 'em the slip. When they passed by— I heard 'em talkin'. I knew they was after me. And they aren't far behind now. (*He looks toward door.*)

ISRAEL: Jim, I can't let you stay here. You'd better get out— quick!

JIM: Why? What's wrong?

ISRAEL (*pointing to door*): Samba Saar. He's killed—in there!
(LISE *opens balcony door, then closes it as soon as she sees* JIM.)

JIM: The African! The man with the earrings?

ISRAEL: Oh Lord.

JIM: That great big boy from Africa?

ISRAEL: Oh, Lord Jesus!

JIM: He was a man. I didn't think nobody could kill him.
Who killed him?

ISRAEL: I did.

JIM: You?—For God's sake—You? You—killed—him?

ISRAEL: Oh, Lord Jesus!

JIM: That man was worth a million of us! No slave's blood
in him! And you killed him! What the hell was the matter
with you? Can't us niggers stick together nohow?

ISRAEL: Oh Lord!

JIM (*opens door, looks in room*): Big old jungle boy lying there
like a baby. Danced yourself to death. Danced right up to
old man Death an' spit in his eye. (*Closes door.*) Death wasn't
big enough to get you alone—face to face. Had to sneak up on
you—behind an American nigger. What you got to say for
yourself, nigger? What did you kill him fer?

ISRAEL: I had to. He'd 'a' killed the Major. I—I got tangled
up. In a second I saw all my life back home—just like a drown-
ing man.

JIM: You killed the best man of us all, for a drunken fool.

ISRAEL: Don't be hard on the Major, Jim.

JIM: We're all too soft. We've got more heart than head.
That's what's the matter with us. (*Advances to* ISRAEL.) Where
is the Major, damn him!

ISRAEL: I don't know. He went out.

JIM: Yeh. Leavin' you to face the music.

ISRAEL: He's comin' back.

Jɪᴍ: Like hell he is. He's beat it. You won't see him again. He's gone—and he's gone for good. It's up to us now, Pal. They'll be after both of us. We've got to stick together.

Isʀᴀᴇʟ: No Jim. You got to get to camp. There's no use your gettin' mixed up in this for me. This place isn't going to see me no more.

Jɪᴍ (*following* Isʀᴀᴇʟ): Where you goin'?

Isʀᴀᴇʟ: Back where all the black folks came from.

Jɪᴍ: Back to Africa?

Isʀᴀᴇʟ: I'm going fishing with Samba Saar.

Jɪᴍ: You mean—you're going—to kill yourself?

Isʀᴀᴇʟ: I'm going to buy me a ticket from old man Death.

Jɪᴍ: Good God, no! You can't! Let's you and me pal around here in France.

Isʀᴀᴇʟ: No—that's all over. . . . .

This, surely, is melodrama if there ever was such theatrical fare; and just as obviously it is melodrama into which both the psychological and social awarenesses of our own day have entered, lending sure motivations and posing newer barriers to confront the characters, barriers which we can comprehend as readily as an older generation nodded quick understanding of the obstacles which confronted, say, Pauline in *The Lady of Lyons*. The resolution likewise, while bringing the reasonably "happy" final scene expected of melodrama, necessarily is motivated by the characters' recognition of social conditions as they are.

169

Between the time of *Goin' Home* and of *Mamba's Daughters*, John Wexley wrote in melodramatic form about the plight of a group of negroes but chose the melodramatic form to present an exceedingly "current" problem and made *They Shall Not Die* a piece of dramatic propaganda around the Scottsboro case. His thesis was stated in the title of the play; he wanted to waken the public to rebellion against miscarriage of justice and betrayal of public opinion through misinformation and lethargy. He showed negro youths terrorized into admitting a crime they never committed; two white girls bewildered into false confessions and then later, aware of the serious consequences of their falsehoods, admitting their perjury. The vocabularies of the underworld and the underprivileged world add a convincing contemporary touch. The play ends on a note of prolonged suspense, with the jury out and the court and the audience waiting. The last line of the play, like the title, is both recapitulation and challenge: ". . . . *they shall not die!*" Characterizations here take second place to a story for theme's sake—melodrama steadfastly upholding the standards and marshaling the audience to arms in behalf of ideals, both noble and sentimental.

Not that propaganda is anything new in American

melodrama. We all know that the all-time record for popularity goes to *Uncle Tom's Cabin*, first done, of course, some years before secession. George Aiken wrote his dramatization around the same type-characters Mrs. Stowe had used in her novel, threading the incidents of the story into a fast-moving scenario of escapes and rescues, in the name of freedom and high humanity. In a day when slaves were actually risking their lives to cross the Ohio, the sight of Eliza crossing the ice with child clasped to bosom was somewhat more persuasive than it is now in a day which has almost forgotten state boundaries and has entirely changed the pattern of human bondage. But if Eliza and the ice would be hard for an audience to take seriously today, little Eva's ascent to heaven—which was guaranteed to leave "no dry eye in the house"—would be an impossible hazard for the producer (unless he were making a period revival). We who make up this year's audiences think, of course, that we are too realistic, too "hard boiled," too scientific and psychological and socially-minded, to swallow such trickery. Yet probably we are merely being true to our day in wanting our own special brand of hocum stamped with our own accustomed sentimentalities and shouting the stock phrases and judgments which fall most readily from our own tongues. Melodrama seems to sense these prides and preferences and to adjust its manners and its tailoring to the perennial change of style.

No play is more up-to-the-minute in reflecting these new attitudes than John Steinbeck's *Of Mice and Men*. In the characters chosen, in the frank vernacular these characters speak, in the theme which runs through the series of stirring situations, Steinbeck's play is so contemporary that not only would it have shocked an older generation but it has the power to jolt some members of an audience today; and indeed characters, speech, and theme are so flavored with realism—and with a sturdy rough beauty—as to persuade (or deceive?) some of us into thinking that *Of Mice and Men* is a genuine, new tragedy. Genuine, Steinbeck certainly seems to be; moving, his story surely is. Perhaps it *is* a tragedy? Tragic flaw; man the pigmy in a relentless universe; inevitable devastating catastrophe? Perhaps. Some feel this way about the story, strongly. But the most persistent labelers are not inclined to think so. They rather readily class as melodrama this story which shares with *Mamba's Daughters* the tendency to utilize a very simple personality as the central character, one for whom the ordinary social standards do not exist but who is himself seen to be the product of the

lack of fine ethical standards on the part of society—
the recognition of which is, of course, a new kind
of standard.

Lennie is a huge hulk of a man, strong enough
to lift a four-hundred-pound sack of grain, tender
enough, in a childlike sensuous fashion, to derive
endless comfort from stroking the soft fur of a dead
mouse in his pocket. His chief characteristic is probably his loyalty to George, whom he follows from
place to place, job to job, trouble to trouble. The
troubles are of Lennie's own making, not George's.
The two men have had to flee the last town where
they worked because Lennie had taken a notion to
feel the soft red silk of some girl's dress. The louder
the frightened girl had screamed, the tighter the terrified Lennie had hung on until George arrived in
time to hit him over the head with a fence picket
and drag him off to hide in an irrigation ditch until
the posse passed them by. After some wandering,
the two arrive at a new job, tying grain sacks for a
thrashing crew. They find their bunks in the bunkhouse and take stock of their fellow-harvesters: Slim,
the tall, tanned, expert driver; Candy, a gray-haired
old man with a stump-arm who sweeps out the
shack; Crooks, the colored stable man, lonely, defeated, sociable; Curley, the Boss's son—a mean little

173

fellow always picking a fight he can win—who has recently married a girl with a questionable past and one eye on a better chance; and other hard-working, directionless wanderers. Lennie has been tutored by George to do no talking and, in case of trouble, to make his way back to the marshy bank of the river where the two spent their last night before arriving at the new job. Lennie carries out his orders, constantly reminded by George's quick, warning eye; he keeps still and he works hard; he even evades a quarrel which Curley tries to pick with him. His aim and ambition, his utopia, is the achievement in real life of a certain story he gets George to tell him over and over—a story about a couple of acres of their own they're going to have some day, a little house, a cow, a few pigs, and—most entrancing to Lennie—a lot of furry rabbits who have to be fed. Some day the two of them will quit their tramping from place to place. George has explained the story countless times for Lennie's benefit.

> Guys like us that work on ranches is the loneliest guys in the world. They ain't got no family. They don't belong no place. They come to a ranch and work up a stake and then they go into town and blow their stake. And then the first thing you know they're poundin' their tail on some other ranch. They ain't got nothin' to look ahead to.

LENNIE (*delightedly*): That's it, that's it! Now tell how it is with us. (*Takes hat off—places it above him on ground.*)

GEORGE (*still almost chanting*): With us it ain't like that. We got a future. We got somebody to talk to that gives a damn about us. We don't have to sit in no bar-room blowin' in our jack, just because we ain't got no place else to go. If them other guys gets in jail, they can rot for all anybody gives a damn.

LENNIE (*who cannot restrain himself any longer. Bursts into speech*): —But not us! And why? Because—because I got you to look after me—and you got me to look after you—and that's why! (*He laughs.*) Go on, George!

So George begins all over again about the rabbits and the garden and living off the fat of the land. If George tells the story often enough, Lennie can work and save his money and keep out of argument indefinitely. As the days go by, Candy is drawn in on the enterprise too. He has money saved up; he'll put it all into the venture. The three elaborate their dream together.

But Curley's wife is no asset to the men's peace of mind. She is always appearing at the door of the bunkhouse "looking for Curley." The men make no attempt to conceal the fact that they prefer their jobs and good pay to her favors, but still she pops up unexpectedly in places where she ought not to be found by Curley. For Lennie, life moves along rather happily after Slim gives him one of the new

Shepherd pups which he can pet to his heart's content out in the barn. Better than a mouse, the puppy is, and not so much danger of crushing its head. George, too, feels better about life; he begins to set stock by his own story of the two acres and the little house; he can no longer spend his money the way the other men do because he keeps thinking how much carrot seed he could buy with each dime. Finally the day comes when he computes that in another month his money and Lennie's, added to Candy's savings, will be enough to buy the place and to make a start. Suddenly George smells the "carnation stuff" that Curley's wife "dumps on herself." She has been eavesdropping. She doesn't like the name she's being called; she doesn't like living here with nobody to talk to and Curley's refusing to take her to dances any more. Her harangue is broken into by the sound of voices approaching. Almost immediately Curley is there. When he sniffs the carnation perfume in the room, his anger bursts into flame. His accusations shift to George; sooner or later someone has to shut him up and George prepares to fight. Lennie, in terror, gives a high nervous chuckle, whereupon Curley turns on him, lashing out with both hands. Big Lennie takes a punishing, tenaciously remembering George's repeated admonitions to keep out of trouble. Suddenly George has had enough, if Lennie hasn't. "Let him have it, Lennie! Let him have it!" he shouts. So Lennie lets him have it, crushing Curley's right hand in the grip of one of his own huge palms. By the time the fighters are separated, Curley has to be taken to the hospital to have the hand saved. The ensuing days make George more wary, Lennie more silent—and more devoted to his pup. They just aren't going to be drawn into any mix-up which will make them lose the pay that will buy the little farm.

One Sunday afternoon Lennie is in the barn dully stroking the body of his dead puppy, which he has crushed with an affectionate "bounce." Now maybe George won't let him tend no rabbits if he finds out the pup got killed. Curley's wife comes into the barn. She hides a suitcase and coat in the grain box; she means to make her escape that night. Then she sees Lennie and knows that he has seen her. She begs him not to tell. They fall into conversation, each talking more to himself than to the other one. She reviews her past life and its disappointments; Lennie talks about his future with George and Candy; outside the men pitch horseshoes. Lennie is nuts, Curley's wife says, not unkindly. No, Lennie insists, he just likes to pet soft things with his fingers.

Things like velvet. He once had a piece of velvet of his own. Curley's wife understands. "A person can see kinda what you mean. Sometimes when I'm doin' my hair I jus' set there and stroke it because it's so soft." Her hair isn't coarse like Curley's, she says, but fine and soft. She lifts Lennie's hand to her hair to "feel and see how soft it is." Lennie likes stroking the soft hair. "Oh, that's nice," he says over and over. His strokes become harder and Curley's wife grows frightened. She screams and Lennie clasps his other hand over her nose and mouth. Now he is twice as terrified as she is; if George hears her making a fuss, he'll be mad and maybe he won't let Lennie tend rabbits. He shakes Curley's wife violently until her neck snaps sidewise and she lies quite still. Then he realizes that something is wrong; that he's "done another bad thing." In a daze he partly covers her with hay, whining pitifully like a child. With the dead pup in his arms he slips off through the door. After the horseshoe tournament is finished, the men find Curley's wife and are sure at once who did the deed. Curley calls for men and guns to go after Lennie. Slim speaks to George quietly. There's no doubt that the broken neck is Lennie's work, he thinks, but they mustn't let Lennie be caught and locked up, strapped down, confined in a cage. That isn't the way for Lennie. Yeah, George knows; and he puts a gun in his pocket.

On the sandy bank of the river Lennie waits for George just as he said he would if he ever got into trouble. Reluctantly he buries his dead pup; there is enough the matter as it is. After a while George finds Lennie and barely has time to hide him when the other men come up. Slim, at a sign from George, misdirects the men down various roads; but they arrange to meet back at the river. When Slim is gone, George calls to Lennie. Lennie wants to go hunting with the men; he likes hunting. But George, rather huskily, orders him to sit down. Lennie senses deep difficulty and begins to plead. "George! Ain't you gonna give me hell?" He wants it like he's always got it before; he prompts George, repeating the words of past recriminations. And then he comes in with his usual refrain: "I can go away. I'll go right off in the hills and find a cave if you don't want me." This time George doesn't rise to his cues. Through stiff lips he assures Lennie gently that he wants him to stay right here.

LENNIE (*craftily*): Then tell me like you done before.
GEORGE: Tell you what?
LENNIE: 'Bout the other guys and about us!
GEORGE (*recites again*): Guys like us got no families. They

179

get a little stake and then they blow it in. They ain't got nobody that gives a hoot in hell about them.

LENNIE (*happily*): But not *us*. Tell about us now.

GEORGE: But not us.

LENNIE: Because . . . . I got you—

GEORGE: Because I got you and—

LENNIE: And you got me and we got each other. That's
what gives a hoot in hell about us.

George goes on with the old story. He has Lennie
sit down by the river and look across; look hard
enough and he can see the little place . . . . a cow,
a pig, and chickens; down in the flat a piece of al-
falfa—for the rabbits—

GEORGE: Right across the river there. (*Slowly taking the Luger
out of his pocket.*) Can't you almost see it?

LENNIE: Where, George?

GEORGE: Over there. You keep lookin', Lennie. Just keep
lookin'.

LENNIE: I'm lookin', George; I'm lookin'.

GEORGE: That's right. It's gonna be nice there. Ain't
gonna be no trouble, no fights. Nobody ever gonna hurt nobody, or steal from 'em. It's gonna be—nice. (*Placing gun at
back of* LENNIE's *head.*)

LENNIE (*happily*): I can see it, George. I can see it! Right
over there—I can see it!

George fires. As Lennie crumples and falls, his
heavy body crashes down a small willow tree. The
voices of the men are heard in the distance—growing
louder, nearer, as the curtain falls.

180

The constituents of melodrama are all here: night under the stars in the woods by the river; a bunkhouse full of hardened men who work largely to forget themselves in an occasional night out; a fist fight which eventuates in the maiming of the Boss's son; a girl of questionable repute who doesn't at all mind losing any man his job; a murder in a stable; a fugitive, a posse, night coming down on the river again; and a final homicide. And yet . . . . we are likely to come away from this play, especially as interpreted by actors like Broderick Crawford, Wallace Ford, and Will Geer, with more feeling for character than for story; and with more feeling for the implications of the story than for the tale itself. Indeed, at times the play does achieve the dimensions of tragedy by sketching behind the individual characters the vast numbers of other homeless drifters who work for a toe hold in a society which really has no place for them. This aggregate of the unwanted becomes a personality which looms larger than any individual —larger and more significant, threatening, pitiable, disheartening. Certainly *Of Mice and Men* is melodrama in the outline and emphasis of its story, but melodrama of a distinctly contemporary sort, with motivated characters who speak for a "problem" which calls forth the sympathy and the intelligence of the audience for its solution. Here again, however, the current ethical standards—at least of that part of society which shares the playwright's point of view—determine the angle of the audience's judgment and the degree of its sympathy.

Probably nothing on the current stage more realistically portrays the difficulties which current melodrama must surmount than Irwin Shaw's *The Gentle People*. In plot the play is melodrama: a gangster holds up two poor old men for five dollars a week in return for his "protection"; he makes love to the daughter of one of the men; plans to abscond with the gal and her father's savings; is trapped by the two old men, knocked over the head, and dumped into the sea. In characterization the play sometimes approaches comedy, as we have noted, with the old men Jonah and Philip rather fully drawn and convincing, struggling with their own natures as well as with exterior circumstance. The rest of the characters are the types of traditional melodrama: Harold Goff, the smart young gangster; Macgruder, the policeman; Florence Goodman, the nagging, complaining wife; Stella Goodman, the starry-eyed, movie-influenced daughter; Eli Leiber, just a plain ordinary youth who loves Stella honestly; a judge who makes the expected decisions against the honest

182

men; a Polack attendant in a Russian bathhouse; a Jew who has lost his money but not his line of talk; a detective who thinks he knows more than he does. These characters say exactly what they should say in order to be "true to life" for the species they represent. Sometimes they are too true to life and seem to be "taking off" the convictions and the actions which are assigned to them; then the play becomes farce and the moments which might have been tensely melodramatic are instead hilariously funny. Fortunately this dramatic composite was bright enough to result in a Group Theatre production, for which they could draw from the ranks such actors as Roman Bohnen and Sam Jaffe to make amusingly appealing a couple of ordinary old men; and from Hollywood a Franchot Tone to give us a suave, slick gangster from screenland, and a Sylvia Sidney to impersonate one of melodrama's sweet young heroines. The playwright seems to sense the confusion he has let himself in for; he prefaces the printed play with a sort of guidepost:

This play is a fairy tale with a moral. In it justice triumphs and the meek prove victorious over arrogant and violent men. The author does not pretend that this is the case in real life.

Now anyone can see that, as a man with a viewpoint on life's inequalities and unfairnesses, Irwin

183

Shaw knows what he thinks; but as a playwright he is in a dilemma. His story might have been straight melodrama of the exciting, realistic sort if he had not let himself become so absorbed in the first act with his two real characters. Or, if he had stuck to the stories implicit in these two characters, he might have worked out a very convincing comedy of the more serious sort. But he had a melodramatic story to be followed and type characters to be moved about in their expected entanglements. Between his two possibilities—comedy or melodrama—the playwright is lost, although not unhappily. The audience are also lost; in the first act they have the emotional response to psychological melodrama if not to comedy, in the second act they are following the unwinding of a typically melodramatic plot to kill a man, in the third act they see the man murdered—and greet the murder with a fine hospitable laugh instead of a shiver of uncertainty. The end of the play is a kind of beaming contentment for all—characters, audience, and playwright. Undoubtedly the playwright will say that this is all as intended: ironic; that the thoughtful overtones should mean much.

But as it reaches us, the story of *The Gentle People* is a cheerful hybrid. Jonah and Philip want nothing in life so much as a little boat of their own in which they might some day make off for the Gulf Stream for deep-sea fishing and freedom. Jonah wants freedom from his monotonous work and his heckling wife; it will be hard to leave his daughter Stella, but after all Stella has Eli, and Eli will make a good husband whenever Stella decides to settle down. Philip wants freedom from his long hours of cooking cheap food in Angelina's restaurant and from Angelina's recent determination to marry him. The two men are saving their money; they have one hundred ninety dollars of the five hundred necessary to buy the boat. And in the meantime they come nightly to Steeplechase pier to sit fishing. The young gangster Goff appears, demanding protection money; he meets Stella when she comes down to see her father, he meets Eli who is with her. He likes Stella, asks her for a date, goes to see her, begins to show her the night life of the city. She is increasingly infatuated with him and his good clothes and his easy money. Her mother's scoldings, Eli's dull resentment, her father's honest warning, are not enough to make her throw off the spell of Goff's attentions. When her father finds that she is about to go off on a trip to Cuba with Goff, he offers her the one hundred ninety dollars of savings with which to take a vacation by herself. Stella tells Goff about her father's offer, and Goff promptly demands this exact amount from the two men in their fishing boat— unless they want their boat in the bottom of Sheeps- head Bay. Jonah grows bold and calls the police. Goff and the two men are taken to court, where Jonah tells their true story. But Goff produces a paper which he had forced the two men to sign at the time they began their five dollars a week "pro- tection" payments; the paper is drawn up as a loan for a thousand dollars, it is legal, the case is dis- missed. Then Goff takes "justice" into his own hands; he finds Jonah alone one night in his boat and beats him with a rubber hose. When able to move, Jonah goes to a Russian bathhouse to get the bruises and stiffness steamed out. He sends for Philip and proposes that they pretend to be friends with Goff, then lure him into their boat on pretext of taking him across the bay, where Stella wants him to call for her. They can then pretend to have motor trouble; Jonah can ask Goff to hold the rudder while he inspects the motor—and Philip can come up be- hind Goff and hit him over the head with a lead pipe. After which, well, they can throw the body into the bay. The plan is agreed upon. There are temporary hitches because of Goff's indecision about

186

getting into the boat and Philip's indecision when the moment comes to wield the lead pipe; but Goff does get into the boat and Philip does get up the nerve to knock him cold. The two old men take Goff's wallet, which contains the hundred ninety dollars he had taken from them, plus the twenty-five dollars for five weeks' extortion, *and* four hundred sixteen dollars besides. They keep the money and throw Goff's body overboard.

It is a week before the body is found and the fact of Goff's death revealed. Stella is taken to the morgue by the police to identify him; it is a terrific ordeal for her. Eli comes to the boat where Philip and Jonah are fishing to tell them about Goff's death; he notices Jonah's wallet and tries to remember where he has seen it before. Stella, too, seeks out her father at the pier; she needs consolation— and Eli furnishes it. Then come the police, along with a detective checking up everyone who has recently had any dealings with Goff. The detective searches the men—Philip demanding to be first because he knows that Jonah has the wallet. When the detective gets around to Jonah, he finds nothing but fishworms in the old man's pocket. Philip cannot understand what has happened to the wallet. After the police have left and Stella and Eli have gone off happily together, Jonah explains: He threw the wallet into the water, but first—he fastened it onto his fishhook! Money in hand, the two men, chuckling, fall to talking of the Gulf Stream, where "the water's warm and the sun shines for eleven months a year."

We can see easily enough that for unity of tone *The Gentle People* does not come off so well. In structure it is more melodrama than not; but it is scarcely an example of swift-moving, entangled, exciting action for action's sake, carrying the gospel of the more intricacies the more tension. Nor is it an example of the present-day psychological melodrama; it hints at a start in that direction, but almost at once retracts the promise. We are given laughs instead. Of course the laugh has always been injected into any melodrama, old or new, because we need a bit of release from tension and also because, particularly today, we want an alibi for our excitement, and what better alibi than the smokescreen of our laughter? Nor can one say that *The Gentle People* propagandizes at all actively on a current social problem, as for instance *They Shall Not Die* fiercely propagandizes. But one thing this play does reflect: the demand put upon any present-day dramatist who essays what used to be called melodrama. He must

188

make his characters convincing; he must show how they became as they are and why they are driven to their desperate acts; he must give them the reactions, the prejudices, and the vocabulary of their time, of their profession, and of their social status; he must hold up ethical standards with which a majority of his audience will agree (the more so if it is a "minority" audience); he must stick to a story which seems plausible. The audience expects all these things of melodrama today because we have been made psychologically self-conscious and sociologically analytical by a generation that has fallen heir to a great deal of amazing scientific discovery which it can neither handle nor get along without. We want all the good things of an earlier day—including unencumbered melodrama—but we also want all the good things of a new day, including fully motivated characters. We cannot be surprised if now and then we get a merry mixture which falls somewhat short both in dramatic structure and in characterization.

IV.

FARCE WITH A PURPOSE

ALL THESE YEARS WE HAVE KNOWN QUITE WELL THAT comedy is something guaranteed to make us laugh, and now along comes the analyzer to tell us that present-day comedy is inclined to back a laugh into a corner for a psychoanalytical interview. Then, not content with showing us that comedies need not be amusing, he proceeds to prove that a lot of plays which we were sure were tragedies are really a very serious variety of comedy. Well, if tragedies are comedies and comedies are not funny, when do we laugh? We begin to be afraid that gayety and joyous irresponsibility are being banished from the stage.

The analyzer hastens to reassure us. If we mean a sort of robust fun, gayety is not gone from the stage because we still have farces, the legitimate descendants of the old-time buffoonery. Our analyzer merely questions whether there is any "irresponsibility" left in them. For even the farce-makers these days seem to wish to be, vicariously, their

190

brothers' keepers. The characters of their plays perform their antics on the slippery floor of social forces and trip up on the banana peel of a Freudian flaw. Scratch the surface of a farce, says the analyzer, and we find that the fun rests upon a foundation of something that is not hilarious; dig deeper and let ourselves *think* about the preposterous maladjustments dramatized at such hilarious tempo, and the farce becomes by implication something very serious, if not in fact a potential tragedy. So what is known in theater language as the "belly laugh" has been relegated to what remains of the vaudeville stage, to a few rough-and-tumble scenes in musical shows, and to the "funnies" of the newspapers and the cinema. Analyzed, most of our farces today are just as funny as a cartoon in the latest *New Yorker* or the *Daily Worker*—no more, no less. The laughs are there, all right; but the laugh comes from our heads. The fun is barbed with social content, the characters are under the psychologist's scrutiny. And so when we go to see a farce tonight we are not quite permitted, as we had hoped, to check all of our logic at the door and climb with expectant diaphragms onto the joy-bus.

Perhaps farce in any day has reflected more of its day than we are aware of now. Perhaps it has always reflected current problems at an absurd angle, like those side-show mirrors which ludicrously distort face and figure when we look into them. Today we are merely more aware of the psychology behind the face and the physiology behind the figure. At any rate we will all agree, audiences and analyzers alike, that the basic elements of farce—fortunately!—have not changed. The characters of farce have to be people we know well enough so that we can get their motivations quickly. In other words, they are types and we enjoy them all the more because "we know someone just like that." Sometimes they say the very things we have heard ourselves saying, brightly or ineptly according to our predicament—or at least the bright things we would like to have said if we could think as fast or speak as boldly in a topsy-turvy situation. Generally, however, they say the things we too have said at some time or other, to our blushing embarrassment, when caught in an absurd situation.

For it is really the situation that always makes the farce: the kind of a fix that people get themselves into. And out of. Certain situations have always been good for a laugh, and always are. Any place, any race, any time. The fall of the haughty, for instance—we like that, it is an outlet for the sadistic

in us, and the stage can be our own harmless in-
quisition. Hottentot chief in full regalia or Middletown banker in his brand new uniform as governor's
aide, the playwright merely has to lift them upon
the stage and exaggerate their dignity a bit and the
audience is gleefully ready, like a firecracker waiting
for the match; ready to laugh as the chief grandiosely
sits on the wobbly lid of his cannibal stew, or the
banker lowers his nice new uniform onto an ice-
cream cone. The playwright likewise has always
been able to get a guffaw from a situation wherein
someone is mistaken for someone else, or a person is
taken out of his element to let us see how he will
act and react in another element, or a more or less
innocent schemer is caught in a trap of his own
setting. Of course *we* would never mistake the ship's
chief steward for its commander or the pompous
secretary for the shy little great man himself; *we*
know what to do with finger bowls and how to eat
artichokes; and none of us has ever overenthusiasti-
cally greeted another's hobby only to find ourselves
the custodians of a Pekinese or the conductor of
someone else's visiting aunt, uncle, and three-year-
old nephew on a sight-seeing tour of the city. If
these situations of farce are trite in the naming, they
are often persuasive when they occur, especially in

the theater, where they have a way of taking us off guard and appealing to our sense of the ridiculous before we have time to remember that they are "old stuff" and we are not really amused. Moreover, while the same basic situations seem to exist from one generation to the next, each new era has its own new materials out of which to contrive the situations and its own timely topics around which to marshal new nonsense. Altogether, perhaps no form of the drama has changed less and still seems more smartly of the moment than farce.

Fundamentally farce may change very little; but in its pattern of dress, speech, and manners it takes on the distinguishing traits of current life. The best mixture for today seems to be one of current patter, reasonably convincing psychological motivation, and realistic setting, blended with a Thought. The compound says something about the current confusions, if not in the form of didactic statement at least in pointed situations devised to pierce someone's complacency. No contemporary farce could be mistaken for the handiwork of any other generation than our own. Indeed, most farces are stamped with the date of their own presidential term if not of their exact year. They are built to be realistically timely. And because of the emphasis upon realism, it is frequently difficult to say these days whether a play is old-style comedy or new-style farce. If our interest lingers with the characters in spite of macaronic absurdities of situation and exciting tangles of plot, then the play is probably—for us, at least—a comedy. But if the characters, although somewhat psychologically convincing, seem less important than their amusing blunders and their successfully scaled improbabilities, then the play is farce for us. Not that it matters, except as it may add to the fun of those who happen to like pasting labels with their left hand while reaching for another laugh with their right.

Clifford Goldsmith writes a play to which George Abbott gives a fast-paced stage career. The resulting *What a Life* is typical of the play which supplies us with hearty laughs along with (or because of?) a genuine interest in character. It is a new farce. Or is it? It may be a light comedy with a knack of putting the boy hero on a spot in order to see him wriggle free in time to get on a hotter spot. The answer depends, no doubt, upon our individual response to Henry Aldrich. If Henry happens to remind us so forcibly of our own younger brother, or of our son, or of ourselves when young that we identify ourselves with his adolescent quandary, then the

195

boy's psychology may outweigh in interest any of the befuddlements he blunders through, and the play is comedy. If we see him as just another typical boy going through this dreadful and amusing business of growing up—and if we feel ourselves safely on the side lines, a trifle proud of what we have outgrown— then the play is farce.

The play begins when Henry is sent to the office of the high-school principal, Mr. Bradley, for having caused a disturbance in his room. He doesn't see how he could have caused a disturbance because he wasn't doing anything except scanning *Hamlet;* someone else might have caused the disturbance falsely accredited to him. But when George Bigelow, who sits next to him, is called into the office, he opens Henry's book to a drawing of the teacher—a drawing which Henry had never in the world intended should look so much like Mr. Patterson! Henry is placed on probation; any more nonsense and he will be suspended. But being in the principal's office has its recompense: Barbara is also there and Barbara is everything that the president of the Junior class should be. Henry admits it; and he asks her to the forthcoming dance. Barbara would like to accept but she has already promised to go with George. However, when George and Henry get into a fight,

Barbara feels drawn to Henry's side and breaks the date with George. Henry is her man if he can find two dollars to pay for the tickets, the carfare, and "fifty cents for emergencies." Henry's mother, Mrs. Aldrich, comes to the school opportunely—or inopportunely, depending upon the point of view— while Henry is still in the office. She wishes to inform Mr. Bradley that, since Mr. Aldrich has recently been elected president of the P.T.A., she feels Henry should be held to stricter standards of scholarship; that is what a school is for. Henry, more interested in two dollars than in his father's Phi Beta Kappa record, approaches his mother for pecuniary aid. His mother will give him the two dollars if he comes through his history exams with the highest grade in the class. So for days on end Henry studies; he studies hard; he chews coffee and sits up late. Finally he takes his exam and might have rated at least a passing grade—except that his teacher happens to notice that his answers to a great many of the questions are exactly like the answers given by George, who sat across from Henry. Put on the spot once more, Henry denies cheating. But when orally quizzed on the exam, he is sadly vague about the answers.

MR. BRADLEY (*holding a sheet of paper*): Would you mind if I should ask you a few questions from this examination?

HENRY: No, sir.

MR. BRADLEY: Who was Marius?

HENRY: Marius? . . . . Marius? . . . . He . . . . How do you spell that name, Mr. Bradley?

MR. BRADLEY: I am not asking you how to spell it. I am asking you who he was.

HENRY (*trying to laugh*): Yes, sir. . . . . Ah . . . . He wasn't a Roman senator, I know that. . . . . He . . . . I know—he was an officer and liked to proceed into battle and he liked to fight . . . . in wars . . . . you know what I mean?

MR. BRADLEY: You are sure he was not a senator?

HENRY: Yes, sir. . . . . At least, the Marius I'm thinking of wasn't a senator.

MR. BRADLEY: What was the cause of the first Punic War?

HENRY: Greed and jealousy and the desire for expansion.

MR. BRADLEY: When did Rome fall?

HENRY: Rome fell—Rome fell in 300 A.D.

MR. BRADLEY: I always supposed that it fell in 410 A.D.

HENRY: Oh, sure, that's right, 410 A.D. But she really started to go all to pieces about 300 A.D.—at least that's the way it seems to me.

MR. BRADLEY: Then why did you put 410 on your paper?

HENRY: Did I put 410 on my paper? Well—I guess that's right, then.

MR. BRADLEY: What territory did Rome rule at the height of her power?

HENRY: Does that mean—?

MR. BRADLEY: It means exactly what it says.

HENRY: Well, there was the city of Rome, of course,—and there was—Don't tell me, Mr. Bradley.

MR. BRADLEY (*throwing down the paper*): I have no intention of telling you!

HENRY: But, gee whiz! I'm all mixed up! I'm not even sure of my own name.

MR. BRADLEY: And you still insist that you received no help?

HENRY: I didn't get any help! I didn't cheat, I tell you. I'm just mixed up!

Mr. Bradley is obliged to conclude that Henry has cheated and must be suspended for sixty days. Meanwhile Henry's latest drawings, which have a way of coming to light at the wrong moment, add nothing to his reputation. But he has one friend at court. The assistant principal, young Mr. Nelson, allows to Henry that almost every man of any ability and ingenuity has cheated at some time in his life; he has done so himself. The point is to discover that it doesn't get a fellow anywhere and then to forget it. Mr. Nelson seems to have a very understanding mind, perhaps sharpened by his own lack of success in persuading Miss Shea, the attractive office secretary, that he would be a fine matrimonial investment.

As if young Henry were not already in about as tight a fix as he can manage—with the dance so near—a pawn ticket bearing his name is suddenly discovered in the boys' locker-room. The pawn

199

ticket leads to locating the three hundred dollars'
worth of band instruments which have recently been
stolen from the school. Henry insists he never stole
the band instruments. But if Henry cheats, perhaps he also lies. The dance is now out of the question; even Henry sees that. He explains to Barbara
that he has to go away; his uncle has tuberculosis out
in Denver and may die any time within sixty days.
Of course the villainous George is not only ready to
take Barbara to the dance but is even now off at the
tailor's having his new tuxedo fitted. With reform
school hanging over Henry's head, he listens rather
more open-mindedly than usual to Mr. Nelson's
views on schools—while the detective is tracing the
pawn ticket and the band instruments. Mr. Nelson
believes that trade school is the place for Henry—
a chance to draw pictures in spite of the fact that the
elder Aldrich was a crack historian and a Phi Beta
Kappa. He goes so far as to bet two dollars that he
can get Henry's mother to consent to trade school.
The detective returns; the name on the pawn ticket
was not in Henry's writing even as Henry had insisted. It is in George's writing. George is brought
in from the tailor's wearing the basted tux which
was part of the pawnshop pay. There being no
tighter places for Henry to squeeze into at the mo-

ment, he is cleared of the theft, acknowledges the cheating, recants on the matter of the dying uncle, receives a couple of dance tickets from understanding Mr. Nelson and permission to go to trade school from his mother, *and* complete forgiveness from Barbara. Then just to keep the audience from looking back reluctantly at any loose ends of interest still unsettled, Miss Shea decides that she might, after all, be able to go to South America with a young man who would rather practice engineering than teach it to high-school students whose assistant principal he also has to be.

Such is the framework of *What a Life*. The old devices of farce: both mistaken identity and the rascal caught in a trap of his own setting. We see the central character shoved from one tight situation to another, without appearing to have much say-so about the shoving. But some of us feel that here also we see a fairly well-motivated study of an adolescent who is defeated by the achievements of his father and bewildered by his own creative gift—a kind of case study in modern education, presented with exaggeration and paced to farce tempo. For some of us the play "says something" to and about parents, teachers, boys; something essentially true for any age and particularly true in an age of regimentation. We laugh,

201

to be sure; the laugh is the play's reason for being; but along with the laugh comes a hint of a thought. . . . . We had forgotten that education—and parents—could be so stupid. And so funny.

As some will wish to call *What a Life* a comedy, or compromise by affixing two labels and stamping it a farce-comedy, so some in every audience will hesitate before Clare Boothe's farcical manipulation of characters and situations in *Kiss the Boys Goodbye*, wondering if she also has not produced a comedy instead of a farce—this time a comedy of manners. Surely farce when it deals with the smart and sophisticated has always veered close toward the manners label; and comedy of manners has always had strong elements of farce, with ingenious plot contrivance and generally, indeed, with at least one highly melodramatic moment; but it has had more intrigue and artifice than either farce or melodrama. We used to be told that a farce may revolve around any sort of characters from any walk of life, while the comedy of manners is sure to have a generous sprinkling of sparkling women whose charm is neither unconscious nor unsought, and that the dialogue of such a play tends to be more brittle, more satirical, more given to epigram than gag. But now that farce has developed a penchant to move into the field of riper

202

characterization, this fast-stepping form necessarily takes on more of the sophisticated flippancy of its haughty sister. Wherefore there is room for the diverging opinions we find concerning Miss Boothe's play. Certainly almost all of us seeing Brock Pemberton's production of the play have the risible reactions expected from farce, and the situations are hilarious as the loquaciously naïve young daughter of the Old South comes up No'th to show you-all that she is the ideal candidate to play the screen role of a typical southern belle in a typically popular romance of the typically glamorous Dixieland. Our heroine!—she says so herself. She is whisked by special train to the country home of a movie producer, where she meets a house party of Westport sophisticates—and also the rather hard-boiled, not quite so young woman who felt that she had the star's part nailed down before the advent of our little magnolia blossom. Naïveté among the intelligentsia; the out-of-her-element formula: farce. Yet this is tuned to brittle dialogue which touches practically all the topics we talk about today, from Hollywood to Washington politics, sex to fascism. The bright lines crackle from all angles of a story framework, including for good measure a thwarted seduction in a moonlit set wherein our heroine's pistol misses the

man but wins the stakes. All of which seems to
sound like the old-time comedy of manners. Miss
Boothe herself steps into any argument as to what
her play really is, to remark that it's propaganda—
something about fascism in these United States. As
if that were a totally different kind of play. Or as if
it mattered what we called it anyway, so long as we
have a good time seeing it.

In *Kiss the Boys Goodbye* the Hollywood ways are reflected obliquely, as it were, from the Atlantic sea-
board. It is natural enough that moving-picture per-
sonalities should have come into all types of plays
in a day when everyone goes to the talkies and talks
so much about them. From Tarkington's and Wilson's *Merton of the Movies* on down through Hart's
and Kaufman's *Once in a Lifetime* the citizens of
Hollywood have gone under the playwright's microscope, not coming off without numerous satirical
jabs but still retaining, for the majority of playgoers,
something of the allure of fabulous inhabitants of
far-off places—even in the land of farce. In that
respect the Spewacks' farce of recent years, *Boy
Meets Girl*, is just another accelerated "inside" story
of the way the films are made. In another respect,
however, it illustrates rather well the frank and
breezy emergence of the subject of sex into the open

air of the stage, which today treats the theme as objectively, and sometimes as freshly, as a crowd of college students at an afternoon tea in the dean's home. Not since Restoration days have plays in English so used the subject for jest and situation. The Spewacks' farce illustrates the easy acceptance of the theme by what is known as the "general public"; most of the matinees of *Boy Meets Girl* were sell-outs. Yet imagine our grandmothers buying tickets for this play, to say nothing of going home afterward to tell the family all about it at the dinner table.

The sex situation, of a kind which in our older drama could scarcely have been told without a snowstorm, is here used chiefly as the springboard for the subsequent action and satire. The action is built to an ancient formula which is, as one of the script-writers in the play states it: "Boy meets girl. Boy loses girl. Boy gets girl." Nothing new about the formula; but the trimmings are something else. The boy in the case is Rodney Bevan, who appears in the casting-director's office wearing what the costume department insists is the uniform of a Coldstream Guard. By his criticism of this uniform Rodney gets himself fired before he can have a chance to prove to his family back in England that he can act. The girl in the case is one Susie, a waitress, who has "the

ineffable charm of touching naïveté"; and she enters
the tempestuous office carrying a tray of food for the
men. Having set down the tray, she serenely faints
at their feet. Being brought back to consciousness,
she asks with her first breath if they have napkins,
and then insists to "C. F.," the director, that she is
quite all right.

SUSIE: There's nothing wrong . . . . it's only natural.

C. F.: Only natural for you to come into my office and
collapse on the floor?

SUSIE: Oh, no, sir . . . . it's only natural for you to feel sick
when you're going to have a baby.

LAW: A baby!

BENSON: Susie, you're not going to have a baby!

SUSIE: That's what they told me. . . . .

BENSON: Susie's going to have a baby!

LAW: Let's get drunk!

C. F. (into phone): Tell that doctor not to come. You heard
me. I don't want him. (He hangs up.) I won't have my office
converted into a maternity ward! (He turns on SUSIE.) I don't
think much of your husband—letting you work at a time like
this!

SUSIE: Oh, but I haven't got a husband.

C. F.: Huh?

SUSIE (rises): You'd better eat your lunch before it gets cold.
Have you all got napkins?

LAW (humbly): The new generation! Faces the facts of
nature without squeamishness, without subterfuge. "I haven't
got a husband," she says. "It's only natural," she says. "I'm
going to have a baby." . . . . . Susie, you're magnificent.

206

Susie: I'm quitting at the end of the week so I thought I'd tell everybody why. I wouldn't want them to think I was discontented.

Law: Our little mother!

Susie: Oh, don't make fun of me.

Law (*rises*): Fun? I've never been so touched in my life. Susie, I feel purified.

Benson: Susie—can we be godfather?

Susie: Do you mean it?

Benson: Do we mean it? We haven't got a baby. And we've been collaborating for years.

Susie: Oh, I think that would be wonderful for Happy to have writers for a godfather.

Benson: Happy?

Susie: I'm going to call him Happy—even if he's a girl. Because I want him to be happy—even if he's a girl.

Benson: Beautiful! A beautiful thought! Where are you going to have this baby, Susie?

Susie: In the County Hospital. It's all fixed. I was very lucky because I've only lived in the county three months and I'm not eligible.

But the jubilant script-writers will have nothing like that. The Cedars of Lebanon Hospital is where Susie will go. Against C. F.'s protests they get the hospital on the telephone, make immediate arrangements. Susie shall have everything that Gloria Swanson had—only double. And as for the bill, why the hospital can send *that* to the studio.

Thus Susie steps into the limelight instead of the

snowstorm; and audiences, like Susie, take the baby in stride. As they take the ensuing absurdities. The baby incident gives the writing team of Law and Benson an idea for a new play needed for Larry Toms, the "western." Larry will find a baby . . . . gambler . . . . Las Vegas . . . . girl leaves baby on ranger's doorstep . . . . Law and Benson are off to write it. Everybody is off except Susie, whom the returning Rodney finds all alone. They talk. They eat. They part reluctantly when others drift in: boy meets, loses, girl.

Presently Susie has her baby. He is a boy and he is Happy. Law and Benson are not only the godfathers, they have the power of attorney for the infant. Happy goes into pictures and makes the big lights, dragging Larry Toms with him. Susie goes to high school to learn so that she can keep up with Happy when he gets to college. She hasn't forgotten the young man in uniform, but she's never seen him again. Success succeeds success! until Law and Benson forget to watch their power of attorney and Larry's manager discovers it has run out, whereupon he sics Larry on to proposing marriage to Susie in order to become Happy's legal guardian. For the child's sake, Susie supposes she ought to accept; she goes to a première with Larry and speaks to the

208

crowd—for Happy's sake—through a microphone. But Law and Benson are busy outwitting Larry and his manager. They have hired a young chap who chanced to drift into the studio—none other than our lost hero Rodney Bevan—to go to the première and greet Susie spectacularly as the father of her child. "Stop! I'm Happy's father!" Rodney shouts to Susie; and into the microphone, "I did not go down on the 'Morro Castle.' I've searched for you in the four corners of the earth. Susie, why did you leave me?" C. F., listening in at his studio, is floored. He knows what the reaction will be "in the sticks." Benson allows, however, that the romantic turn of affairs will send Happy's stock up a hundred per cent. Meanwhile everyone is hunting Susie, everyone is hunting Rodney. Susie finally appears to announce that Happy is in the hospital with measles; Rodney is found locked up in an office and insists that Law and Benson gave him his piece to speak over the microphone. Whereupon Law and Benson are fired, peremptorily and finally. But they are not the last of C. F.'s worries: Larry appears—with the measles; he caught them from Happy. Nor are the Benson and Law worries over: Happy's star has set when he is still only eight months old, for Larry's manager has got a new idea to replace Happy—a baby contest. Moreover, C. F. and the powers higher are dickering with Gaumont-British to buy out the whole studio. Being without funds and not knowing where to borrow any more, Benson and Law have an idea. They go into Larry's hospital room after he has been wheeled off to his sunbath and use his telephone to call a friend in Paris, persuading him to cable from London in the name of Gaumont-British raising the ante on the studio from three million to five. They are charging the toll to Larry just as Larry comes back.

> LARRY: What's the idea of using my phone?
> BENSON: Do you object?
> LARRY: Certainly I object. I ain't gonna pay for your calls.
> BENSON: All right, if that's the way you feel about it—here's your nickel.

Excitement in the studios next day; the cable from London offers the five million on condition that the entire studio force be signed up—except Larry Toms. Into the jolly commotion comes Rodney, bringing flowers for Susie and wanting to marry her. His visa has expired; he has to leave for England and wants Susie to go along. Susie demurs. He doesn't know about her past. When she tells about it, Rodney finds—as we do—that it was all pretty much on the square; she married a bigamist by mistake. In brief, the good old new standards upheld just as the good old standards used to be. So Susie is free to marry, all right, but does she want to marry? After all, who is Rodney? Whereupon, to answer the question most effectively, in comes the true representative of Gaumont-British, who of course happens to know all of Rodney's distinguished family (We guessed it!)—his father, Lord-This, and his sister, Lady-That, not to mention his brother, Captain Bevan of the Coldstream Guards. The offer cabled from Gaumont-British may have been phoney, but not Rodney's family, or his devotion. Boy gets girl.

In this way the contemporary farce is built on a theme which is reasonably convincing, in a setting which neglects nothing in apparent verisimilitude, with characters who seem fairly lifelike snapping smart comebacks in the current slang, while the whole admixture reflects the standards of the day. All through the play, situation shares the spotlight with clever dialogue; but it is not the kind of dialogue which develops full characterization. When Benson and Law are at their epigrammatic heights, nothing is really happening to them, or to anyone else, because of what they are saying. Talk for the sake of more and better hilarity; action for the same good reason.

As everyone knows, *Boy Meets Girl* is far from being out of the ordinary merely because of its taken-for-granted attitude toward sex. Nor is the subject an unusual one for farce. Farces and comedies, in one way or another, have always added their share of commentary to the general subject. Whether Wycherley speaks through *The Country Wife* or playwrights of our own generation like Catherine Turney and Jerry Horwin speak through such a play as *My Dear Children*, these lighter forms of drama hold up a mirror for each generation to see its own attitude toward the perennial problem of relations between the sexes. Naturally if a playwright emphasizes the sex problem until he demands our thoughtful attention, the play will be in consequence an extremely serious one. But if the playwright prefers correction through laughter—or laughter without any notion of correction—or has a story in which bumptious action speaks louder than the best of dialogue, then he is likely to marshal his situations in farce formation. And our playwrights, like our educators and pulpiteers, have indicated a growing insistence on taking sex out of mysterious corners. On the stage the sly whisper has gone the way of the snowstorm.

There are certainly no mysterious corners in *My Dear Children*, and as John Barrymore romps through the farce there are a good many lusty laughs. The "children" of the title are grown up enough, all of them, to carry their end of the sophisticated dialogue and situations.

According to the story, Allan Manville, somewhere along in his late fifties, is an actor of some distinction: his *Hamlet* is known to two continents— as is his private life. At present he is on a somewhat extended vacation in the borrowed castle of his erstwhile friend Ernest Van Betke; "erstwhile" because Manville has met Van Betke's inamorata, the beautiful actress Felice, Countess de Britonne, and carried her off to the borrowed castle after a spectacular fray with Van Betke which made newspaper headlines across Europe. The fight seems to Manville's valet to have been a little unnecessary considering the fact that Van Betke was on the point of backing Manville in a huge theatrical venture in America. As Manville and the Countess return to the borrowed castle, their motor car breaks down and the Countess is sent ahead, arriving to find the castle full of reporters seeking a scoop on the fight. Among the reporters is a persistent but shy young lady, Portia Trent. When Manville arrives, he manages to dismiss all of the reporters except Portia, who demands a few minutes alone with the actor. Then shyly but with genuine concern for his well-being, she tells him that she is his own daughter. When Manville finally takes in the fact that he has a daughter so grown up, he is much pleased to have her visit him right now when it is Christmas time and families should get together. He remembers her mother well—an actress. Portia is no actress; she is a physicist studying at Cambridge. Moreover, she is interested in a young man, Lee Stevenson, who sees in her only a friend. Manville promptly wires the young man to come for Christmas; calls the Countess to meet his daughter and prepares for a grand celebration. But Portia is not his only surprise for the day. Miranda Burton, starry-eyed and seventeen, likewise arrives—having run away from boarding school—and announces herself as another daughter. The newspapers have given her a clue to the whereabouts of her distinguished father and she has come for the Christmas holidays. Ah, but of course, Manville remembers *her* mother very well—a sculptress. He is charmed to have Miranda; he introduces her to her half-sister, Portia, and to the somewhat astonished Countess. Then out of the Christmas snow comes a third daughter—Cordelia Colby, most beautiful of the three daughters, most disillusioned, and most like her father.

The house party gets under way when Lee Stevenson arrives, a smug little chap who promptly falls for the glamorous Cordelia; and then comes handsome Willard Nelson, who once jilted Cordelia and now wishes he hadn't. Miranda chooses to fall madly in love with Willard, who rather leads her on. A costume party brings all the family and guests together, including Jacques Korby, famous inventor whose technical language Portia understands. A lesson in makeup and come-hither from her father makes a different girl of Portia; she out-glamors them all and finally goes off to Paris with the inventor. After Miranda's own particular brand of heartache is more or less healed by the knowledge that Willard has a wife at home, she cables her mother in the States that she is thinking more favorably of the home-town boy she met "under a boat." Cordelia has the bitter pleasure of refusing Willard's offer of marriage, after he shall divorce the girl who originally came between them. The Countess leaves in several kinds of a huff; even the privilege of marrying Manville and becoming the mother of all his charming daughters is not enough to hold her. Besides, says she in final anger, she herself actually precipitated the whole affair—love, fight, and flight—in order to break off the friendship between Van

215

Betke and Manville. Only Cordelia is left, but she orders her car and then before getting into it gives her father a first-class piece of her mind: they are alike, Cordelia and Manville; they understand each other, the old roué and the hard young daughter. Van Betke returns with his men prepared to throw Manville into the icy river; let him swim if he can. Still jaunty and defiant, Manville is nevertheless a sorry figure: no money, no job, no daughters, and not much chance to survive the river. But once more Cordelia appears in the doorway, all calculated charm for Van Betke. Yes, he will help with her stalled car. Whereupon Manville, in final banter, breaks into one of his most famous scenes. Cordelia picks up the cues—and in no time they are disagreeing on interpretations. Van Betke is pleased, amazed, excited. Cordelia is the leading lady they have been looking for! She shall play opposite her father on the grand American tour. And so Manville need not write his memoirs—yet. Life lies ahead.

Here are the exaggerated situations of farce with their sudden laugh-provoking turns of action—the irate Manville, for instance, putting Cordelia across his knee for an old-fashioned spanking; the Countess waiting in the conservatory for her ardent lover,

216

who is too busy making spaghetti sauce to remember
the rendezvous; the half-thrilling, half-absurd threat
of a revolver in Manville's always histrionic hand—
these are planned and paced for the laughs. If there
is much reality in the fun, it is achieved chiefly
through the sense one gets in performance of the
spontaneous fun Barrymore is having, as if this were
really his borrowed castle and these his daughters,
and in the neatness of characterization also accom-
plished by Doris Dudley, Lois Hall, and the piquant
Dorothy McGuire. If the play is typical of its year,
though built on the sound stuff of all the good old
farces, it is in the matter-of-fact way in which the
situation is set up and solved; playwrights of a few
years ago might have felt it necessary to bring Allan
Manville into an Indian summer of benignity,
much as the English Pinero felt compelled to reform
his gay Lord Quex to meet the mores of the nineties.
If the play has a "lesson," this lesson is so contemporary that we may miss it.

Just as *My Dear Children* makes its commentary on
sex for the oldsters, so Mark Reed's *Yes, My Darling
Daughter* has a thought about the youngsters. Or is
it a thought about the older generation's thought
about the youngsters?

The darling daughter of this piece is Ellen Murray,

217

a distinctly attractive girl of twenty-two, whose father is Lewis Murray the banker and whose mother is Ann Whitman Murray, that feminist leader who helped break the shackles for women back in the days when Greenwich Village was busily setting up new standards. Ellen has an interesting aunt also, Constance Nevins, her father's sister, just now returning from Reno after her third divorce. Fresh out of college and looking for a job, Ellen makes it her business to get a first interview with the new house guest, a Mr. Jaywood, who happens to be an important literary agent. She is, she explains to him, guaranteed not to fall in love and not to be compelled to leave a job within a year because she is going to have a child; definitely, she is a career woman. So she says. And then, while she is still talking to Mr. Jaywood, along comes young Douglas Hall, to explain to her as soon as they are alone that he didn't attend her commencement because he was broke. But now he has given up architecture; what's the use of working at a profession which after six years of study and work won't pay a fellow enough to go see the girl he loves receive her diploma? So he's landed himself a selling job instead. He's sailing Monday night for Belgium on a two years' contract. He hadn't meant to say so much but since he has

218

. . . . . well, they are both ecstatically in love, aren't they? and it's only two days before parting . . . . for two years. Therefore, says Ellen promptly, she is not going to Hartford to a house party as planned; she is going with Doug for the two days. "Somewhere! Some little cottage maybe . . . . with a lake and a canoe. We could cook our own meals, and smoke and talk, and plan our whole life together." Doug demurs; it isn't his idea of a good start but Ellen insists that her plan is "an emergency measure"; it's their chance. Besides, she knows that her mother would not object if she knew about it because her mother has always been "tremendously advanced."

While Ellen is off to pack, Mother Ann and Mr. Jaywood renew an old acquaintanceship of which they are saying nothing to the family. Aunt Connie flutters in to impart the information that she has a sure intuitive hunch that Ellen is not going to the house party but "off somewhere with this boy"; she's seen Ellen repacking her bags, riding breeches instead of party dresses, her eyes shining and starry. Ann knows the idea is preposterous; in fact she knows her daughter; but she goes upstairs to ask a few questions. Alone with Ellen, she asks the questions and gets honest answers. Ellen is going away with the man she loves; she cannot marry him and two years

219

is a long time. Ann's arguments sound sentimental to Ellen; they aren't logical. Reaching for a little book of poetry, she reads her mother a poem out of her mother's past—those days on Barrows Street when John Bliss was "the coming young poet of the era." She draws a colorful and accurate picture of those halcyon days; and to her mother's sharp question as to where she heard so much, she explains that she did a thesis for Senior English on "The Contribution of Greenwich Village to the Cause of Freedom in American Art and Morals." There is a difference, Ann insists; *she* was an independent reporter on the *World* at twenty-two, while Ellen is dependent on her father, who most certainly will not approve. But Ellen is going anyway; regretfully, hating to hurt her mother, assuring her that she will be back on Monday—if her mother and father want her back. There is a last-minute compromise. Ellen will bring Doug in to meet her mother; they will have tea together, including Mr. Jaywood in the party. Just before she finally goes, Ellen has a moment alone with Mr. Jaywood, whom she has figured out to be the missing poet of her mother's youth. Then she goes off bearing, if not her mother's approval, at least her wistful blessing. When Lewis Murray comes home, the tempo changes. He senses that there is more to his daughter's week-end than he is being told; Connie drops hints, Ann is too calm. When he pieces together the story, he is bitter. His father told him twenty-five years ago not to marry a woman with a past; now he's reaping what he sowed. Angry, unhappy, and on the verge of tears, the capable, efficient, "advanced" Ann Whitman Murray cries, "Oh, goddam sex anyway!"

On Monday morning Ellen comes home. Happy. She is going shopping with Doug while he gets a few last-minute things. But her father has a different idea.

LEWIS: You two are both deeply in love, aren't you?

ELLEN: Of course we are. (*Indignantly*.) What do you think?

LEWIS: I think maybe I can help you.

ELLEN: I don't know what you can do . . . . unless you start rebuilding the economic system, and a lot of people are ahead of you on that already.

LEWIS: Have you considered marrying this Mr. Douglas . . . . ?

ANN (*helpfully*): Mr. Hall, Lewis.

LEWIS: Mr. Hall . . . . before he sails?

ELLEN: Of course I haven't! We don't even dare consider it until after he gets back.

The telephone interrupts this exchange of ideas; a call for Mr. Jaywood from the *Paris Herald* office; they feel over there that they can find a position for the young woman Jay has told them about. The news suits Lewis, who can now state his own plan: a quiet little family wedding at Greenwich, a nice quiet little supper which "your loving mother will arrange," and then Ellen and Doug can be off on the "Queen Mary" at midnight. Neat, isn't it? Very neat—except that Doug is sailing steerage on the "Laconia." Moreover, Ellen will not accept a bridal suite for a wedding present. She will not hang herself on Doug's neck and she won't have her father support her after she's married. A job, yes; but nothing more. When Doug arrives, Lewis is not in an easy mood in spite of much cautioning from Mr. Jaywood. He lets Doug know that he knows where Doug and Ellen spent the week-end. Then the ire is no longer one-sided. Does Lewis mean that *he* knew and Ellen's *mother* knew and still *they let Ellen go?* Well, Lewis himself didn't know, he says, until after they'd gone.

Doug (*thoroughly mystified*): But Ellen assured me . . . . why, we all had tea together . . . . nobody knew then.

Jay: A few of us were in on it.

Doug: Did Mrs. Murray know?

Jay: Oh, definitely.

Doug: Before we started?

Jay: Yes.

Doug: Do you mean to say that Mrs. Murray sat there all the time, served tea and talked nonsense . . . . ?

JAY: That's right.

DOUG: Did *you* know?

JAY: Oh, yes!

DOUG: What kind of a family is this?

JAY: They're extremely nice people, Mr. Hall.

DOUG (*to* LEWIS): Say, why didn't some of you raise a row? Then, naturally, I wouldn't have thought of going.

LEWIS: Not much courage, eh?

DOUG: Oh, I've plenty of courage. I admit if a person didn't know the facts, my conduct might seem kind of rotten; but frankly, I think you have only yourselves to blame. You know I'm beginning to get pretty good and sore about this!

LEWIS: By God! *You* needn't get sore . . . . !

Then everybody is sore. Ellen at her parents for letting on to Doug that they knew; Doug at Ann for calmly serving tea and letting her daughter go. Doggedly Doug insists that the family listen while he proposes to Ellen. And Ellen refuses. She'll sail on his ship and see about her job and then maybe—

DOUG: Ellen, I'm sorry. I can't let you take the same boat with me. . . . .

ELLEN: Why not? You didn't buy it, did you?

DOUG: Ellen, you and I are going to be married here, right now, today, where your family can watch . . . . or you're not going to see me for two years. . . . .

ELLEN: Darling, you're just having a moral spasm. It'll pass.

But it's now or never, says Doug firmly. Then it's never, says Ellen just as firmly. And so they part,

223

Lewis' blessing on Doug. But Ann Whitman Murray, the bold crusader of the Greenwich Village era, has a "pleasantly vigorous" word to say to her darling, and baffled, daughter.

> I think, when a man makes such a fuss over being seduced
> . . . . a nice girl ought to marry him. (*It is the tiny fillip needed
> to decide* ELLEN.)
> ELLEN: Maybe you're right. (*Calling.*) Doug! Doug, wait
> a minute! (*She turns and runs out.*)

Naturally, farce must end on a happy note, and this certainly seems like one. A final moment as idyllic as a pastoral, a solution as moral as any sentimental comedy could wish. The story, nevertheless, is the brisk, brusque romancing of a very present-day generation, and the play says something with its laughs: it is all very well for mothers to advocate deep-sea swimming for women but when their own daughters are ready to wade out it's "Yes of course, only you mustn't go *too* far out."

But if we are looking for a moral in a farce, for a real spiritual boost wrapped up in the cellophane of a jolly philosophy, we might as well turn at once to that Pulitzer prize-winner of the same year, *You Can't Take It With You.* This is indeed sentimental comedy gone farce, and it is easy to understand the concern for the state of the nation's drama which was aroused in the minds of some persons when the sages of Columbia awarded the prize to Moss Hart and George S. Kaufman for their dramatization of a national Urge To Be Cheerful. For this is hokum, timed to the theatrical minute, boldly and boisterously executed, and—what seems worst of all to the objectors—spotted with moments of apparent sincerity and even "feeling." No evident shafts of satire in this, as in *Susan and God*, Rachel Crothers' comedy on the same general theme. While differing opinions still reverberate, we can always take a look at the Hart-Kaufman piece for ourselves.

Among present-day farces, none is more patently absurd and hilariously preposterous. It is the story of a household which couldn't possibly be like that. And yet to many in any audience it is more persuasive than most farces. Persuasive because, without staying its fierce tempo, it makes them feel that they are getting glimpses into the inner nature of the characters. Characterization? Of course not, really; yet the members of this wild household do seem to reveal themselves, so deft is the playwrights' sketching of them, until there comes a kind of recitative spell in the midst of hilarities when the onlooker is made to feel that after all these people are a little wistful as well as absurd. In this peculiar effect the

225

work of Hart and Kaufman illustrates a marked tendency to be seen in a number of farces of today— the tendency to sink a shaft, as it were (geographically toward the end of the second act) into a deeper level of character interest. The mirth stands aside for a moment and something almost poignant, too swift for tears and too sentimental for intellectualizing, comes to the fore. This nuance of seriousness is the reverse of tragedy's old use of the comic. The older writers of tragedy protected the sensibilities of the audience by giving strained nerves a chance to relax in laughter; the new writers of farce give hilarity a chance to relax in an instant's quiet perception. Then the audience can laugh again with renewed gusto, having been given a sort of second breath for merriment. An extra quality of persuasiveness in performances of this play undoubtedly came from actors seasoned in the timing of these nuances as well as in the pacing of straight farce. There were, for instance, Henry Travers and Josephine Hull to interpret Grandpa and Penny, and also former leading stage figures like Mitzi Hajos and Virginia Hammond, the latter being succeeded in the role of Mrs. Kirby by the Charlotte Walker whose name some years ago used to be up in Belasco lights to guarantee, so to speak, the full romantic flavor of an offering like *The Warrens of Virginia*. Indeed, the techniques of the past had a good chance to show, in this one production, that they could adapt themselves to the current methods.

The philosophy of *You Can't Take It With You* is stated plainly in the title; a "thesis," really, if so dignified a term may be applied to an idea which is as much mood as thought. It was Grandpa's idea.

.... Thirty-five years ago he just quit business one day. He started up to his office in the elevator and came right down. He just stopped. He could have been a rich man, but he said it took too much time. So for thirty-five years he's 'ust collected snakes and gone to circuses and commencements.

The whole family are that way. They do the things they hanker to do, instead of just hankering. Their side lines are their main lines. When we have met the family we practically know the story, for the story is just the family going on being themselves in all sorts of strange juxtapositions. The family (and therefore the play) consists of: Penelope Vanderhof Sycamore, known as "Penny," a comfortable, round little woman in her fifties who writes plays "because eight years ago a typewriter was delivered here by mistake"; Paul Sycamore, Penny's husband, who maintains a youthful air well into middle life and manufactures fireworks in the basement; Essie, daughter of the Sycamores, now in her late twenties, who dances for the love of it but makes candy for sale as a side line; Ed Carmichael, Essie's husband, who composes for the xylophone and sells Essie's candy—each box with a neatly printed quotation from Trotsky or someone else who has caught Ed's fancy; Alice, young, fresh, and lovely, who works down town and has a slightly practical air which does not make her any less charmingly a member of the family; Rheba, the colored servant, and her friend, Donald, who is always at hand to assist with the work, although not for pay because he is on relief; Mr. De Pinna, serious, bald-headed assistant in the manufacture of the fireworks. And Grandpa. Grandpa is about seventy-five if one insists upon being statistical, but he is youthful and wiry and exuberantly at peace with the world. The household revolves about Grandpa as naturally as spokes about a hub. On the other hand, the plot, such as it is, revolves around Alice because Alice is interested in a young man who is interested in her—Anthony Kirby, vice-president of Kirby and Company—the boss's son. "Just like the movies." Tony comes to see her and meets the family; and he's shocked in spite of all her warnings, but he's pleasantly shocked.

However, Alice refuses to let him marry into such a "cock-eyed" family.

> ... I'd want *you*, and everything about you, everything about *me*, to be—one. I couldn't start out with a part of me that you didn't share, and a part of you that I didn't share. Unless we were all one—you, and *your* mother and father—I'd be miserable. And they can never be, Tony—I know it. They couldn't be.

Just by way of proof, she invites Tony's mother and father to dinner. They come, but come a night early, when the house is at its maddest: a slightly disheveled actress, cordial but rather drunk, is asleep on the living-room couch; a Russian ballet dancer who wrestles as a side line—with the guests—assists in doing the honors; each member of the family is doing his own particular stunt—typing, dancing, making fireworks, or caring for snakes, as the case may be. Not a successful evening, and climaxed by sudden arrival of the police. They have come to search the house, and they don't like what they find. So the entire party lands in jail. Why? Well, Ed has taken to printing subversive sentiments on the candy cards; it isn't that he cares about the sentiments, but he likes to print things. After their release from jail next day, the senior Kirby comes back to call. The Grand Duchess Olga Katrina is already there; the Grand Duchess has "not had a good meal since the revolution" and she has come with the wrestler-dancer Kolenkhov for dinner, forgetting her job in Child's for the ecstatic pleasure of making blintzes for the family. Grandpa and Mr. Kirby exchange philosophies in the interest of Tony's and Alice's future happiness. Mr. Kirby wants to know what he is expected to do; live the way Grandpa and the rest of them do—doing nothing?

GRANDPA: Well, I have a lot of fun. Time enough for everything—read, talk, visit the zoo now and then, practice my darts, even have time to notice when spring comes around. Don't see anybody I don't want to, don't have six hours of things I *have* to do every day before I get *one* hour to do what I like in—and I haven't taken bicarbonate of soda in thirty-five years. What's the matter with that?

Mr. Kirby thinks it is a ridiculous life; he is not aware of missing anything in his own life; moreover, Grandpa's philosophy is dangerous, "it's un-American." And that's why Mr. Kirby is opposed to this marriage. But his opposition does not restrain Tony's appearing in order to restrain Alice's disappearing. And the end of the matter is that they all have dinner together with stacks of blintzes for all.

If the main plot is skimpy, the stunts and byways of stage business and dialogue do a generous job of feathering out. There is the case of Grandpa and

230

the federal agent who comes to collect his back income tax which Grandpa has not paid since 1914. Grandpa does not intend to pay it; anyone who wants to can pay for Congress and the President, but not Grandpa; except maybe seventy-five dollars. Grandpa's attitude is all right with us, and we do not object when the tax-collector has to shout over xylophone music, dodge snakes, and jump at the blast of a new bomb firecracker banging off in the cellar beneath him. Indeed, when there is a chance of any lag in interest in *You Can't Take It With You*, there are always the firecrackers to go off, solo or ensemble. All in all, a mad family; and a mad idea to try to make a play of such complete nonsense. To accomplish it, the playwrights have managed to stir up all the ingredients of farce in this household, and flavor the mixture with an essence of sentiment; so that, strange as it seems afterward, in every audience some heads beside Grandpa's and the family's are bowing mentally when this family and their assorted guests sit down just before the blintzes are brought in and the old gent taps on his plate for silence before he begins his friendly and respectful remarks to make the tag of the play.

Well, Sir, here we are again. We want to say thanks once more for everything You've done for us. Things seem to be

231

going along fine. Alice is going to marry Tony, and it looks as if they're going to be very happy. Of course the fireworks blew up, but that was Mr. De Pinna's fault, not Yours. We've all got our health and as far as anything else is concerned, we'll leave it to You. Thank You.

Almost all the way through this farce, as through other farces, we laugh. That's what we came for. Not to solve any of our problems, but merely to expose ourselves to the release of laughter. Indeed, if we think of the theater at all in terms of our own problems, it is usually only to pick one of these rollicking plays and decide to "laugh it off"; although what sometimes happens is that we are able to laugh ourselves into a sense of proportions. The absurdities upon the stage serve as a sort of social safety valve, an antitoxin which we can receive painlessly and more or less unconsciously.

Most plays in these days—comedies and melodramas as well as tragedies—depict the social order as mowing us down or propping us up, and emphasize the kind and variety of this new Fate with which we have to deal. Farces, on the other hand, have a way of depicting the funny pigmy man as taking his Fate too seriously. They restore a sense of human importance, not by dwelling upon the roots of character motivation but by showing us how many circumstances are not important. We spend an evening with these plainly preposterous Vanderhofs, watching them on the stage daring hard-masked Fate and getting away with it, and we come out of the theater feeling of course that the Vanderhofs are burlesquing life, but feeling also that maybe we are bungling life a bit ourselves. Almost any good preacher, priest, or practitioner might tell us the same thing; but we are constitutionally inclined to combat precept and argument, whereas farce catches us off guard.

So this least august among the forms of drama shows up the social order by showing up the foibles and banalities of those who make up the social order. Dealing with man generically, by type rather than by arresting individualization, by cartoon rather than by candid camera shots, a farce can make its point without apology or explanation, and certainly without making us too self-conscious as we watch it. As long as man can take time out of his jostled, frustrated, and frequently too earnest days to go to a theater where a farce is playing, there is a chance that the distorted social order is not congealed into its mold past all refashioning. As long as a man can laugh, he feels that there is hope not only of life but of thought. Even, sometimes, of action. "Laugh it

233

off," we say. Today's farce-makers often go further and say, "Let's laugh it *on*." They tickle us into laughing with them. About national affairs, local affairs; about public characters, our neighbors, ourselves. Perhaps if we know what a nation is laughing about, we know what it is thinking about. We may guess tomorrow's headlines . . . . and day-after-tomorrow's footnotes. . . . .

V.

TO THE LEFT, TO THE RIGHT, OR YOUR OWN WAY OF THINKING

TECHNICAL TERMS FOR CLASSIFYING ALL PLAYS HAVE largely gone from our vocabularies. Some of the words, like "tragedy" and "tragic" in particular, seem to have been taken over by the writers of newspaper headlines; and when we do use such terms ourselves, it is likely to be in the same loose fashion. In our conversations about the theater we scarcely use them at all. We are not concerned with technicalities and would hate to be asked, offhand, to define the terms; and if we did try to define them, no doubt someone would at once disagree with our definitions, just as we disagree with the definitions of others—and sometimes with our own. We have easier terms for our theater language today. From the theater itself we have picked up the expression "show business," which surely is broad enough to satisfy any unmeticulous person; and the shows of the show business may include anything from puppets to a spectacle, from Lunt and Fontanne in Chekof to Beatrice Lillie in a new revue. Being a little more specific when commenting casually on plays, we talk of "dramas" and "comedies" and "musicals." And everyone knows what we mean: a drama is a serious play, a comedy is an amusing play, and a musical is a musical, from *Knickerbocker Holiday* to *Hellzapoppin*.

We also speak sometimes of going to see a "propaganda play." This, as we all know, is another of the current playgoer's current terms. It is used at least as frequently and as easily as the others; the only difference is that we are not so sure of getting agreement when we use it. What is propaganda to some of us may be the art of realism to others; and what is art to one person may always be a pain to someone else. So although we use the term freely, we use it with varying connotations. If we heartily approve of some particular propaganda play, we are likely to avoid the term when we speak of it. We say, "It's a play with an idea, all right, and pretty cleverly done." Then we chuckle. It *is* clever, we think, to get an idea across under guise of a gripping story. But if we do not care for a propaganda play and are inclined to believe that "if it teaches a lesson it isn't art," then we are likely to say, "It's rank propaganda!" All in all, the word "propaganda" is not in happy repute with the general American public today. It sounds dictatorial to some and "red" to others; it smacks of spoon-feeding, of having our fare chosen with regard to our health instead of our taste. Some of our distrust of the term—frequently our rebellion from it—stems from too many experiences of having uncovered the hocum behind alleged facts. We live in a debunking age, and "Oh yeah?" comes readily to the lips of this generation. What we want, we tell the world, is unbiased truth. Objectivity is the passion of current idealism. We like to feel that we are the heirs of scientific exactitude, of truth for truth's sake, and let the chips fall where they may. We are, we say, the world's first fearless realists. We've been taught that experience is the thing; take it straight, undiluted; the trick is to make sure you get it all. And so we rebel at the very notion of anyone's picking out the facts we ought to have. Moreover, not only the scientific tradition but the democratic tradition is against our approving anyone's selecting the point of view which is "good" for the people. Let us hear all sides, we say, and we can make up our own minds—our forebears did it in 1776 and we've had a century and a half of training in democracy's hard school.

237

These are the things we *feel* about propaganda. Besides, we are not entirely free from the conviction that changing one's mind is essentially a precarious process. We don't really like to do it. The very acknowledgment that we may have been mistaken yesterday throws doubt upon today's judgment. May tomorrow then reverse the hard-won convictions of today? Better to take our stand by our emotional hearth-fires and look askance at any stranger who comes knocking at our doors with the express purpose of changing our minds. In the end, as in the beginning, we don't like to be told what to do, off the stage or on, and we are inclined to label what we don't like as "propaganda."

But when, actually, *is* a play propaganda? Prejudice aside, there are some plays which we agree are propaganda no matter how skilfully they convey or challenge our convictions. Literally, as we all know, "propaganda" merely means an effort to gain support for an opinion or a course of action. In that sense, we all spend a good part of our lives propagandizing. Most of the time we can *see* more than one point of view on almost any question, but we *prefer* a certain point of view. It is the view which seems to us to give the proper accent to experience. There is usually one way of life which seems best to us—at least best *for us*. And so we persuade toward acceptance of our way of life. Perhaps in so doing we are arguing only for the validity of our own personality; the only way we are ever able to say things, in the theater or elsewhere, is our own way. Thus every play advances the viewpoint, the ideas, the personality of the playwright and therefore has at least some faint element of propaganda. The playwright may be conscious only of trying to persuade us to the illusion of his characters and his scenes. This sort of inevitable persuasion must be the basis upon which some people maintain that all art is necessarily propaganda. As long at it so difficult to separate an individual's way of life among his fellows from persuasion of his fellows to another way of life, it is pretty hard to determine how much propaganda there must be in a play to make it a propaganda play. Most of us feel that a play is a propaganda play when the playwright shows a definite and emphatic intention to influence us to thought and, if possible, through thought to action. In recent years the American theater has had a goodly number of such plays, including a few that are significant contributions to drama as well as to a cause.

Since we have all seen such plays and experienced

239

the fact that they are both good theater and sound argument, it no doubt beggars the point to wander into the ancient discussion as to whether definite, active propaganda belongs at all in art, although it is always interesting to juxtapose the frequently quoted opinions of Flaubert, on the one hand, and of Bernard Shaw, on the other—Flaubert, who would seem to wish us to be aware only of the miracle of imagination created before our eyes and ears; and Shaw, who would have us keenly, alertly aware of the purpose behind the work of art. But, far apart as Shaw and Flaubert are, there is a common denominator in their views, for one notes that Shaw emphasizes the "example of personal conduct" on the stage. And personal conduct means *characters in action*, and characters in action mean *story*, which is of course the imagination of the playwright creatively at work. The props of the propaganda play are always characters in action, in turn holding up the thesis with which the audience may find a convincing measure of identification.

The place where out-and-out propaganda plays bog down, including Mr. Shaw's, is at the point where characters cease action and the stage becomes entirely a rostrum—call it a "pulpit" or a "soapbox" as we choose. Audiences know by instinct that dogma has to be derived from experience, not experience from dogma, and they have to see and feel the experience occurring upon the stage before they can arrive at the playwright's dogma. Indeed, completely to accept the playwright's argument, audiences must receive it emotionally to such extent that they are not consciously aware of his logic until after the play is over. At an effective propaganda play audiences are always caught—perhaps unconsciously—in the struggle between the centrifugal force of social theories and the centripital force of human interest. Some persons would rather hear characters upon the stage discuss ideas than see the characters being affected by the ideas in terms of life situations. Such people are "naturals" for the consumption of spoken propaganda. Most individuals in an audience, however, are primarily concerned for the characters in the play: What makes them as they are? What will they do with the circumstances in which they are caught? Can they really do anything? When the characters begin to *do*, to master their circumstances or to be mastered by them, then the play, including its propaganda, takes on life. Whether the characters of the play are the figures of realism or of dramatic abstractions, we catch that quality of theater which is necessary to all drama only if the

241

characters move before us in convincing action. And convincing action means action with which we are emotionally identified: vicarious experience. Understanding the necessity for being swept along emotionally with the play's inevitable unfolding, we understand again what Dumas *fils* meant when he said that the art of the drama is the art of preparations, and that a play is the shortest route from emotion to emotion. Whether we agree or do not agree with the thesis behind a play which thus persuades our imagination, we are caught at attention. We cannot immediately deny our experience. And so there is a chance—a chance at least—that the playwright may be able to persuade us to both thought and action.

Eugene O'Neill furnishes a fair illustration of this sort of persuasion, particularly since we do not usually think of him as a propagandist at all, except that when O'Neill has something to say he makes every endeavor to say it effectively. Sometimes the quality of his "thinking" may seem mediocre; he may appear to flounder in a sea where cross-currents of thought confuse his sense of direction. When he becomes too conscious of such attempted thought, sometimes symbolized by masks and dual identities, he cannot steer a straight course for port, and we do not follow him eagerly. In plays like *The Great God Brown* and *Days Without End*, O'Neill the dramatist is interrupted by O'Neill the would-be philosopher of a none-too-lucid philosophy. Probably the only time that a dramatist dare philosophize is when he is so sure of his own philosophy that none of his characters need be self-conscious about it. But when we look at *The Hairy Ape*, although the play is symbolical and Yank an abstraction, we have a direct emotional reaction. The characters, although symbols, are struggling, suffering, moving in action. Hence some of O'Neill's "message" comes across. He himself has said that *The Hairy Ape*

was propaganda in the sense that it was a symbol of man, who has lost his old harmony with nature, the harmony which he used to have as an animal and has not yet acquired in a spiritual way. Thus, not being able to find it on earth nor in heaven, he's in the middle, trying to make peace, taking the "woist punches from bot' of 'em." This idea was expressed in Yank's speech. The public saw just the stoker, not the symbol, and the symbol makes the play important or just another play. Yank can't go forward, and so he tries to go back. This is what his shaking hands with the gorilla meant. But he can't go back to "belonging" either. The gorilla kills him. The subject here is the same ancient one that always was and always will be the one subject for drama, and that is man and his struggle with his own fate. The struggle used to be with the gods, but is now with himself, his own past, his attempt "to belong."

In presenting his philosophic conception of man's struggle with his own fate, O'Neill has not left it to the characters to deliver perorations on the subject; he has taken care to see that they express themselves in motivated action. In fact, the original idea for the play came to him, he says, from a concrete situation.

I shouldn't have known the stokers if I hadn't happened to scrape an acquaintance with one of our own furnace gang at Jimmy the Priest's. His name was Driscoll, and he was a Liverpool Irishman . . . . the synonym for a tough customer. . . . . Driscoll came to a strange end. He committed suicide by jumping overboard in mid-ocean. . . . . Why? It was the why of Driscoll's suicide that gave me the germ of the idea. . . . .

No doubt drama has always been, as O'Neill says, "man and his struggle against his own fate." We do not need to have him remind us—because it is constantly dinned at us from all sides—that Fate today is not the gods of ancient days but some aspect of the social order, some psychological flaw within us. Perhaps the flaw—and hence the Fate—was planted into our glands by heredity and nourished in the field of environmental influence. At least this seems to be our steadily growing conviction, via the science laboratory and the psychological interview, until now we are inclined to say that character isn't "what we're born with" so much as "whom

we're born from" and "what we're born to." When
we feel sure, or too sure, of these present-day con-
clusions as to causes and effects, then the Social
Order becomes deified and drama, reflecting the dei-
fication, is bound also to reflect with increasing intensity the struggle with this new Fate.

The people who appraise this Fate as most of us
appraise it and meet it in the manner we would meet
it are, generally speaking, what we call the middle-of-
the-roaders. They walk with us. At each side of us
are the left-wingers and the right-wingers. Sometimes, of course, we admit to being serenely off on
the extreme right or proudly out on the extreme left.
But more often we feel that we have chosen the best
going, rather near the center of the highway, and
we look askance in both directions. The leftists are
the group we usually think of as propagandists, although this is hardly a fair judgment, because those
on the right are just as keen to bring their own views
to pass, or to prevent others from bringing *their*
views to pass, as the most left of the leftists. Moreover, the rightists are just as prone to deal directly
with the social order.

Because of the impingement of social demands upon all phases of life—it may be more accurate to say
because of our keener awareness today of such im-

245

pingement—we find that in reality all of the plays which we have been discussing carry their weight of social thought to greater or lesser degree. It is easy to see these elements, to the degree of propaganda, in a play like *Awake and Sing*, because Fate, in guise of the social order, is the direct object of Ralph's struggle. He knows that he is smothered under a weight of economic inequality which he cannot lift and from under which he has only the slightest chance to escape. His grandfather sees the threat of defeat even more plainly than does Ralph himself; he not only has had longer experience with the palpable abuses of a system which seems to him to be loaded against the average individual's success, but he also knows that daily routine and the increasing responsibilities of marriage and family will dull whatever edge of adventure the boy now has. Jacob bets his life on what seems to him to be Ralph's one chance. At the end of the play we feel that Ralph has grasped his chance, not in the exact way the grandfather planned, but nevertheless as a result of Jacob's influence. And yet it is only a chance for Ralph, not an assurance. The economic order is still Fate with the upper hand.

In another kind of play which we have discussed, such as *The Silver Cord*, it is less apparent that Fate is operating through the social order. However, social and economic circumstance must have had a large hand in making Mrs. Phelps the particularly possessive person that she was. A harder life might have taken some of her attention off the minutiae of her sons' lives and given both David and Robert a chance at freedom. Wider social contacts, more touch with people of varying backgrounds, might have made her see herself and them with some perspective. She was biased and son-centered partly because she lived in what is sometimes characterized as "stuffy middle-class circumstances," and not entirely because of her love-starved marriage. Not that harder or easier circumstances would necessarily have changed her nature, for we find her counterpart in all walks of life; but that a genuine struggle for economic necessities might have given her a feeling of dependence upon her sons' economic success, and this might in turn have resulted in respectful agreement with their plans or even in catering to their wishes. Also, given economic need, she might have urged Christina to go on with her own work in order to add to the family income. On the other hand, Bessie Berger, if she had led a less harassed life, might easily have been as possessive a creature as Mrs. Phelps. As it was, Bessie did pretty well in

247

dictating marriage to Hennie and in breaking up Ralph's love affair. She had the same complex as Mrs. Phelps about having given her life to her family; but because Bessie Berger had to work harder in order to buy food and pay rent, she could not devote all her energy to managing the lives of her children. In both plays the social order operates, explicitly or implicitly, as Fate. Odets was zealously conscious of the social cause of the maladjustment in the family he chose to show us, while Howard took for granted the cause of the maladjustment in the Phelps family. The left-wing critics will feel that a play like *The Silver Cord* lacks the proper emphasis on social cause; propaganda for the individual is there nevertheless, since Howard makes a forthright example, in Mrs. Phelps, of what a mother wants to steer away from. He utilizes correction by example just as firmly as does Odets; he happens to approach his problem from a different angle.

Propaganda is not absent from the other recent family plays. *Family Portrait* shows up the close-knit fabric of society in which the individual family cannot escape the judgment of the community; economic success rises and falls with social approval. *The Little Foxes* speaks the playwright's mind on the ruthless ways of industrialism and makes Regina almost a personification of the relentless push of a new economic order just as it allows the new protest to speak through the uncertain young Alexandra. Both women are the results of different aspects of the same economic order. Even the happy family of *You Can't Take It With You*, absurd as they were, might be said to be partly the result of economic-social circumstances. The money-mad, success-chasing world was too much for Grandpa. A brainstorm swept him out of the dizzy superstructure of society and made him a propagandizer for the good old doctrine of *carpe diem*. To be sure, he didn't mount a soapbox and begin to shout for freedom; he just went around being free. (Fortunately he had income enough to do this on!) The old gentleman expanded in his freedom in such an arresting manner that the most casual visitor was startled into an ague of questions. Whereupon Grandpa, given a direct opening, had his speech all ready. As Grandpa went, so went the family—all the Vanderhofs were propagandizers for a new way of life which in itself spoke against the customary slavery to domineering Society. A brave and flippant gesture in defiance of Fate-the-Social-Order—if you happen to have enough coupons to clip to keep the fateful wolf off your own doorstep. Some persons may find in this

249

play a stimulus to break their own shackles of slavery
to routine; others, from whom the pinch of necessity
is never far distant, look upon the cheery lesson of
the play as so much sap.

Some playwrights depend upon the flippant gesture to make their point; upon the indirect word or
a laugh where an outcry might be expected. Others
not only state their thesis in so many words but itali-
cize the words. The picture they draw is black and
white, no nuances. In *Dead End*, for instance, Sidney Kingsley shows us poor children all of whom
have elements of nobility and rich children all of
whom are "bad." Inferentially the present economic order has blasted the chance of these poor
children and has made them "good," at the same
time that it has made the rich ones bad. At any
rate, the dice are loaded by the playwright, and
audiences know they scarcely have a chance to exercise their own skill—for judgment is surely a skill
and one which every man likes to pride himself upon
being able to exercise if he can only have his facts
"straight." Some plays are persuasive only to those
already persuaded.

Of Mice and Men is a "social" play in that it depicts through specific individuals the whole group
whom they represent, shows something of how they

came to be as they are, and suggests something of
their inevitable defeat. To a point some will feel
that this play is obvious propaganda. It persuades
to thought. But it does not take the next step and
suggest the action which should follow the thought.
The story is left yeasting in the minds of the audience. *The Gentle People* likewise provokes to serious
thought both through its sincerity and through its
hilarity, but arrives at no Q.E.D. beneath which
audiences must either affix their signatures or else
sidestep a civic duty. *No Time for Comedy*, which
may seem to lean in any direction except left, is
nevertheless a commentary on the social order and
has a generous assortment of satirical jabs to right
and to left. The characters, every one of them, are
products of that element of society which takes a
kind of opiate satisfaction in analyzing how they
and everybody else got to be as they are. Neither
economic nor political conditions force them to do
anything in the way of militant action against any
injustices of their generation. Still they are aware
that, as Bernard Shaw says, "You must either share
the guilt of this world or go to another planet." In
the end it is the perspective which society has afforded them that they give back to society—through
comedy, the social stabilizer. They make their reply

to Fate-the-Social-Order which made them, and make it with a disillusioned epigram.

So, whether any specific playwright may be called a propagandist or not, the shadow of present-day problems and confusions broods over the characters he creates. Whether in a contemporary indictment like *They Shall Not Die*, coming out of a present-day situation of public controversy, or in a contemporary tragedy like *Daughters of Atreus*, going back to the figures of Greek mythology, it is Fate in the form of the social order which is being questioned. Of course there has been a growing tendency all through the century to question things, from the Square Deal to the New Deal, until the most emphatic questioners have moved over far left, perhaps pushed there by the others who have kept on getting more and more "liberal"—though, as we know, it is persistently debated whether the liberal forces have really *pushed* the radicals further left or whether the radicals have *pulled* the conservatives at least to a point nearer center.

Some of the century's furor of questioning is no doubt brought about by the mechanics of technological advancement which have made the interdependencies of living more evident. Some of the questioning is the product of amazement over the

252

paradoxes facing us in our new world: enough food for all and yet starving millions, a passion for peace and yet mobilizations for war. But as soon as one begins to describe our world in terms of its social and economic patterns, he is using words which themselves carry an emotional freight of propaganda. Often the same word carries almost as many different kinds of freight as there are listeners, and each person will label the package of ideas he receives under cover of that word a different kind of propaganda. Some part of every audience sees *Abe Lincoln in Illinois* as propaganda from the right: a restatement of caution in the midst of confusion, a warning to maintain equilibrium for the ship of state. Others in the same audience listen to Lincoln's defense of the textile workers of Massachusetts and acclaim him as a prophet for the left. In just this fashion the audience takes its propaganda to the play as well as receiving propaganda from the play. If the playwright speaks his mind with any certitude at all on any issue which affects us all, someone is ready to call his play propaganda.

No doubt the out-and-out propaganda play rises from this feeling of certitude. Its playwright sees a problem with such ardent conviction that there can be no doubt whatsoever in his own mind and he

253

strives to leave no doubt in the mind of his audience. His plea is direct, heated; his story is flashed in blacks and whites. Although he may not be able to say exactly how the problem is to be solved by society, he knows passionately that some solution must be found, somewhere, and as soon as possible; and his zeal, if it does not overreach itself, may catch on to an audience's emotions and thence to their thoughts, impelling them to attempted action. An audience moved toward action is the hope of all propagandizers, and the most vehement of them employ this direct method. Another playwright, however, may see the problem just as clearly but present it with sorrow and even bitterness, leaving us with a sense that he himself considers any solution hopeless; that indeed, as one of Maxwell Anderson's characters puts it, "the rats inherit the earth." The former method essays to show up something at the white heat of indignation; the other method points out in sorrowful resignation. A comparison of the two approaches may be made by placing *Gods of the Lightning*, which Maxwell Anderson wrote with Harold Hickerson in 1928, beside *Winterset*, which Anderson wrote alone in 1935. Each is an indictment of "class justice"; each stems from the Sacco-Vanzetti case. *Gods of the Lightning* is direct, emphatic, partisan.

Winterset is less heated, less immediate, apparently does not hope to stir audiences toward an indignation which they should try to "do something about" as soon as they get out of the theater. Persons who prefer the one play have little patience with persons who prefer the other. Many feel that *Winterset* is really the more effective propaganda "in the long run"; that the realizations brought to them in part through this one play will make them more clear-seeing citizens hereafter, at the polls and in the jury box, for instance. To which those who prefer the method of *Gods of the Lightning* retort: What is the use of being stirred emotionally if the will-to-do is not directed into specific, immediate channels? These protestors are for the passionate single-track issue which may result in one wrong righted now. But the other group draw back from the too sure answer. Some are fearful of being railroaded into action; some are skeptical as to whether all the cards are actually on the table; some are merely temperamentally slow in reaching a decision. With so many kinds of people to be propagandized, we will undoubtedly continue to have several kinds of propaganda plays.

It would be easy to say that when the facts are distorted and the play too partisan the drama suffers

255

and the propaganda with it, except that the most successful of propaganda plays looms up to confront us, the long-lived *Uncle Tom's Cabin*. It is hard for today's audience to say why the older play was so effective and John Wexley's *They Shall Not Die*, about the Scottsboro case, less effective. Can it be because the audiences who rejoiced in the appeal to humanity which they felt in *Uncle Tom's Cabin* were not drawn from that part of the country which felt any immediate threat to white supremacy in the freeing of the negro slaves, while all parts of the country today feel the economic threat of negroes who can demand their rights as workers as well as citizens? Just another indication, the left-wing commentators may say, that the further removed from our purses, the more acceptable the propaganda. Or perhaps there is a simpler answer in the fact that *Uncle Tom's Cabin* presents a "heroine" who is both rich *and* good (the not yet outgrown dream of most of us) and a protagonist who gives his life for the great and simple virtues of loyalty, honesty, and integrity which we yearn to have (other) people give their lives for. Furthermore, the implied solution of Mrs. Stowe's problem was relatively simple: free the slaves. She did not push her solution for its implications, nor did the audiences push the implications; whereas

Wexley presents a complicated solution which implies freeing the courts from social pressure and freeing the administrators of justice from economic preferment, which in turn means. . . . . But even when audiences are not sure what it means, they sniff the wind of public opinion for scent of danger in the offing.

Many of the older plays spoke to the individual conscience primarily and to the social conscience indirectly. Today's plays have less zeal for reforming the individual. They are sure that we "sin by syndicate." The slogan of the contemporary propaganda play is therefore "Get Together." It wants us to do something about the ills which threaten to engulf society—including ourselves. Ralph says it in *Awake and Sing:* "Get teams together all over." Agate rouses the workers to shout it in *Waiting for Lefty:* "Strike, strike, strike!"—a mass answer to a mass problem. Of course it is easier to escape individual responsibility for a corporate sin, but at the same time it is less easy for the individual to escape the judgments of relentless Fate when he feels himself dependent upon the efforts of the group of which he is a part.

No subject of immediate deep concern has more stimulated playwrights to make appeal to the social

257

conscience than the subject of war between the nations. This subject shares with that of labor's problems the major attention of our socially minded writers. We may wish to add to the list the problems of the family, of youth's desperate necessity to find its way in a disturbing new world, and of the relationships of man to woman when many of the old moral fiats are being re-examined, if not frankly discarded. All these subjects—labor, the family, youth, sex— are of course in one way or another interrelated; and all of them are necessarily interwoven into the pattern of war's demands and devastations. Inasmuch as each of these subjects is universal, each has caught the attention of dramatists through the centuries. In plays that cry out for the abolishment of war the style of arms may change, and geographical locations, and names of gods and imperatives; but the underlying motivation remains the same. No present-day playwright has challenged the devotees of Mars more sharply than Aristophanes challenged them. He chose in *Lysistrata* the method of poking robust fun on a grand scale, to be sure, but his ringing indictment has reverberated into our own decade. The same gales of lusty laughter do not sweep through Robert E. Sherwood's *Idiot's Delight*, with its sharp propagandizing against forces said to breed our wars, such as jingoism, treaties, and munitions plants; yet audiences came away from performances of that play not only with a picture of a world on the brink of being blown to chaos but also chuckling over the antics of a sextette of dancing girls and puzzling over the amusing enigma of where, precisely, Harry Van first met the worldly-wise Irene. It may even be that the word Sherwood wished to say about the wholesale horrors of war does not stay with us so long as the contemporary portraits brought to life by Alfred Lunt and Lynn Fontanne; on the other hand, it is possible that his word will linger because of their portraits. Laughter is not absent from Paul Green's attack on war in his earnestly satiric extravaganza, *Johnny Johnson*, with its score by the expatriated Kurt Weill. Like a bitter comic strip with music, this work has some of Aristophanes' gusty lampoonery along with caricatures so true that they are poignant, although Green's play ends, similarly to *Idiot's Delight*, on the eve of catastrophe, Johnny's boy-scout grandson explaining that "Daddy says we're in for a terrible war and all the people have got to be ready to keep the enemy from destroying us."

When George Sklar and Albert Maltz wish to probe the subject of war, they are altogether earnest

259

in presentation as well as thought, and in *Peace on Earth* argue from a specific conviction that war is the inevitable outcome of a social system based on the profit motive. They focus their thesis on the career of an economics professor, Peter Owens, who becomes involved in a strike of longshoremen who refuse to load munitions for the next war. Peter's best friend is shot in an effort to break the strike, and Peter himself is implicated in a killing at a mass meeting on campus. He is sentenced to be hung for murder, and in his cell the events of his harried and jumbled life pass before him: What is the sense of his struggle when the system is loaded against him? As the curtain comes down he hears the band playing; men are marching to the war he has given his life to try to avert.

Irwin Shaw utilizes fantasy in the guise of realism in *Bury the Dead*, which is timed as occurring during "the second year of the war that is to begin tomorrow night," and which has as its principal characters six corpses who stand stiffly silhouetted against the torn battlefield. No military pomp, as this play begins, about the burial detail digging a trough for six soldiers, two days dead; only chill darkness and stench. A priest and a rabbi pray over the bodies after the dead soldiers are thrown into the open grave; their prayers are answered by groans from the grave. Before the eyes of the horrified soldiers the dead men stand up in their graves, refusing to be buried. The sergeant calls the captain and the captain goes to the generals: six dead men who won't be buried are a problem in military strategy; also in discipline and public morale. Even when the doctor makes official examination and swears the corpses dead, they will not lie down in their graves. Even when the generals prove it their patriotic duty, the dead will not be buried. The generals are gravely explicit.

.... Gentlemen, your country demands of you that you lie down and allow yourselves to be buried. Must our flag fly at half-mast and droop in the wind while you so far forget your duty to the lovely land that bore and nurtured you? I love America, gentlemen, its hills and valleys. If you loved America as I do. . . . .

But the men do not lie down. They have been sold out "for twenty-five yards of bloody mud," which is nothing to die for, they maintain. The consternation of the press, the threats of the business men, the persuasion of the priest, the publicity of the broadcasting system, all prove of no avail. Finally the women are called, the women who have loved them in life and can be counted upon.

Women are always conservative. . . . . The women'll fight the General's battle for them—in the best possible way— through their emotions. . . . . It's the General's best bet. . . . .

So the General addresses the women on their sacred duties, and the women talk with their dead—wife, sweetheart, mother, sister, the women who knew them best. They argue a bit, but understanding steadily draws these men and their women closer; the women comprehend the things the men wanted to live for, the simple human things that should have been their heritage; now the men are dead and the women can only "sit at night with nobody to talk to." The episode of the women blacks out as one of them is shrieking, "Tell 'em *all* to stand up! Tell 'em! *Tell 'em!*" Thus the women are no help to the General, who admits as much, but "for God's sake keep it quiet." Quiet? Reporter, editor, news-boy, voices of the people, take up the outcry. A banker calls the War Department on the telephone, he calls Congress, he calls the Church. "Somebody do something." No one can. And when the General finally calls for men to mow down the corpses with gunfire, the live soldiers refuse, defying court martial.

Be careful, General! I may take a notion to come up like these guys. That's the smartest thing I've seen in this army. I like it. . . . .

And when the General mans his own gun, it is to
no purpose.

The CORPSES *begin to walk toward the left end of the grave, not
marching, but walking together, silently. . . . . Calmly, in the face of
the chattering gun, the* CORPSES *gather on the brink of the grave, then
walk soberly, in a little bunch, toward the* THIRD GENERAL. *For a
moment they obscure him as they pass him. In that moment the gun
stops. There is absolute silence. The* CORPSES *pass on, going off the
stage, like men who have leisurely business that must be attended to in
the not too pressing future. As they pass the gun, they reveal the* THIRD
GENERAL, *slumped forward, still, over the still gun. There is no
movement on the stage for a fraction of a second. Then, slowly, the
four* SOLDIERS *of the burial detail break ranks. Slowly they walk,
exactly as the* CORPSES *have walked, off toward the left. . . . . The*
THIRD GENERAL *is the last thing we see, huddled over his quiet gun,
pointed at the empty grave, as the light dims—in the silence.*

Out-and-out propaganda, of course, presenting the
playwright's protest to a universal problem in mood
and with something like a specific solution.

Such a protest, with its intense purpose as well as
its semi-expressionistic technique, is a very different
sort of thing from *What Price Glory?* the first of our
"realistic" war plays, which still holds up well in
reading and in acting through the gusto of its story
of the feud between Captain Flagg and Sergeant
Quirt and the power of its vernacular dialogue.
There were many in 1924 who saw *What Price Glory?*
as definite propaganda against war; today, now that

263

the surprise of its dialogue has disappeared, most of us recognize the play for what it is—a vigorous story with sharp characterizations, actually a swashbuckling yarn brought down to date—and therefore not differing from the traditional pattern of war plays so much as it was thought to differ when it was first produced, inasmuch as war, for all its sordidness and terror, still remains the romantic adventure, to which Flagg and Quirt ebulliently return as the curtain falls. It is less plausible to think that an average youth, seeing such a play, would become meditative over the evils of war than that he would, like Sergeant Quirt, be unwilling to miss the excitement if others were dashing into it; in short, that the youth would, like Quirt, want the others to "wait for baby." If Maxwell Anderson and Laurence Stallings were propagandizing when they wrote this play, the propaganda was doubtless for freedom to use on the stage the free speech which men (and sometimes women?) speak in everyday experiences. If so, they were propagandizing effectively; telling a story which swung its message along with the story, through the characters that made the story. And today this story stands up strongly in contrast to the polite, if sometimes poignant, *Journey's End*, whose mimic detonations of war sound mimic indeed as Mr. Sherriff's play is revived at a time when Siegfried and Maginot lines make the dugouts where soldiers talked of school spirit and *Alice in Wonderland* seem as remote as the walls of Troy. Aside from possible differences between an American soldier's point of view and a British soldier's, the two plays offer a chance to compare methods of dramatizing for the stage, if not new methods of propagandizing from the stage. Indeed, as propaganda neither play would qualify, because each is, when sufficiently scrutinized, essentially romantic.

Possibly it is because they do not feel equal to proposing specific answers that many playwrights make their protests against war indirectly, threading the protest into dramas on other themes. No one would call *Family Portrait* or *Daughters of Atreus* an anti-war play, they are not even propaganda plays in the generally accepted meaning of the term; yet each incorporates some caustic dialogue on the subject. Not that their authors are expressly making a flank attack on war, but rather because in writing on any pressing theme it may be almost impossible for the playwright with a contemporary outlook to avoid some reflection of the martial distress that clouds this day.

An encouraging sign for propagandists, and for the

265

American theater, is the appearance of the left-wing revue, of which *Pins and Needles* is of course the first outstanding example. That it followed the arrestingly "different" staging of *The Cradle Will Rock* may easily have helped to give this satirical frolic of the Ladies Garment Workers a boost into popular attention. The reactionaries and the middle-of-the-roaders have been far out in front in this matter of persuasion by ridicule. Now that the leftists are beginning to fight back with the same merry guerrilla tactics, the fun ought to be greater for all audiences. The result is likely to be the same process we have noted in the "legitimate" drama, a pulling of many of the more standardized musical entertainments a bit further off center—and, conversely, a pushing-back of some others toward their home base at the right, in stubborn resistance to the newer attack. Again, fun for the audiences, both ways. We shall be able increasingly to choose where to go to laugh at the things we want to laugh at—with always the hopeful chance that some of us may get into the wrong show by mistake (or by invitations which we can't decline) and so be exposed to the open winds of opinion which we are always seeking, theoretically, but not always finding time to expose ourselves to voluntarily. In this way we will be more sure of discovering what the other side finds so funny in our convictions. Even the American theater is a good deal of a democracy.

It requires, of course, a degree of adulthood in any society to laugh at a predicament which includes ourselves. It requires, too, a degree of security. Not economic security and certainly not the belief that the *status quo* is permanent; but security in the resources of personality to make as much adjustment as may be necessary, plus faith in the integrity of personality which cannot compromise too far. "Correction through laughter" is an old device, and one which flourishes best where the democratic idea flourishes. The Greeks were adept in the dramatic technique which makes a public abuse or a puffed-up demogogue the object of unbitter laughter by showing the people as really masters of their masters. Even Socrates, both revered and feared, could be represented in a play as swinging in a basket out over the heads of an audience, the lampoon Socrates popping caustic comments on actors and spectators alike while the real Socrates, sitting in the audience, could profit by the mood and the applause of the people. The Chinese are said to have corrected more than one Son of Heaven by burlesquing his petty officials carrying out his royal reform edicts till they worked absurd hardships on his loyal subjects. No ruler can with dignity weather a nation's loyal laughter; better to re-form his unpopular reforms.

In our own country, legislative chambers and campaign platforms have known this device of deflating by laughter, and it is probable that more than one ambitious but vulnerable "friend of the people" has been laughed out of a presidental nomination. And upon our stage, correction by laughter may sometimes make a stronger case than can correction by heated argument. Moreover, real laughter rides highest and sinks deepest when the characters upon the stage are not all the brittle wisecracking sophisticates who watch life as a passing parade. Nor need laughter be loud to be most effective. In *Pins and Needles* we scarcely laugh at all at the "Sunday in the Park" number. It is partly humorous in a quiet way, and partly—on the surface—just another "pretty" and tuneful interlude. But beneath the surface, like Noel Coward's jazz-craze thrust in "Dance, Little Lady," it throws into quick highlight a present-day condition. "Sunday in the Park" may be better propaganda than some of the fiercer satire in the Garment Workers' revue and is surely more effective than a bombardment of gags. One way or another, we have all known the experience of having only one holiday and then having—rain. Funny, of course, but. . . . . So we who have, after all, some place else to go when it rains, immediately reach into our pockets for another holiday to give "the people"—having been part of "the people" for at least the lifetime of a tuneful production number— and so the producer is justified in his song-and-dance propaganda. This correction-through-laughter method has most chance of being effective when the laughter is not embittered. In *I'd Rather Be Right* the audience may participate in every smart comment hurled in from the right; but when the curtain falls on George M. Cohan doing his fumbling best to serve the people in his humble capacity of President, a share of the audience are leaning *for the moment* a trifle left of center in their identification with the mimic-President's predicament. To be sure, after they have left the theater these members of the audience may have a second thought—or a first thought —and conclude that the play was too true to be really funny. If so, the playwrights have merely proved that ridicule is the subtler propaganda.

Although we can seldom say that their plays are subtle, the left-wing writers have been showing a tendency to tell their purposeful stories with less vehemence and less obtrusive preachment, shifting

269

their emphasis from compelling argument to impelling character, relying more and more upon the
social implications of the stories to speak for themselves. Writers like Albert Bein and John Howard
Lawson have given some promise of tending in this
direction, while we have seen Irwin Shaw coming
again into the theater with *The Gentle People*, so
patently different from *Bury the Dead*, and Odets
returning with *Rocket to the Moon*, which is scarcely
recognizable as the output of a special pleader for
the left and certainly is not tempered to the heat of
Waiting for Lefty or *Till the Day I Die*. It happens
that *Awake and Sing* is both propaganda and a better
play than Odets' later offering; but in the story
of the Bergers he illustrates, perhaps not too consciously, the principle upon which propagandists
now appear to be working: that it is characters in
situation that must carry any thought they have to
give us. It is precisely because Odets has been able
to make the characters of this early play so real, as
we have already noted, that the result is not only a
fine drama but an effective instrument for stimulat-
ing attention to the inequalities of our social structure. Without the one we could not have had the
other. For whatever else may catch our attention,
a good story is sure to. When it comes to welding a

270

group into one mind, one mood, one impulse, a good story has all the power of a pertinent slogan plus the fanfare of a band. A story can dissipate prejudice—or, unfortunately, build up prejudice—where the most logical arguments are ineffectual. As we remarked at the beginning, the important thing for the playwright is being able to create a story upon the stage.

If some of these changes are coming about in the drama of protest, as changes are coming about in other types, what kind of plays are emerging? We may ask the question, but it is one which cannot readily be answered until it can be answered in the past tense. At some future date, perhaps not too distant, we may be able to look back and remark easily, "The fourth decade of the twentieth century saw a marked trend toward. . . . ." Or it may be that we shall comment retrospectively, "The fourth decade was a tangle of unsure philosophic tenets, mixed political dogma, untried economic theories, and adolescent psychology." Whether the tangle is to remain a tangle or to resolve itself into some sort of American design depends upon the sort of playwrights who are emerging. If today's playwrights merely record the current confusion, then their plays will pass. For authentic reproduction of confusion

271

through the medium of an art form is possible only to a mind which senses meaning beneath the confusion, which sees a whole beyond the part. Even if future decades may decide that a man was mistaken in the meaning which he found, the fact that he had perceived total relationships beyond the partial scene will give his work the persuasion of perspective.

Now of course for a playwright to step forth and aver that he has found meaning amid the turmoil which has confounded the bravest thinkers of his day would be to seem altogether too presumptuous except that the playwright is saved by having to express his meaning in terms of human beings in plausible situations; and the need for so expressing himself necessitates his pronouncements' being stepped down, happily, to a degree of familiarity which seems reasonable to his audience. Otherwise he is like an artist who paints the likeness of a skyscraper for savages who have never seen any dwelling but a grass hut or any picture but a crude outline of man or beast. At first, as they gaze upon the sophisticated picture, they see only splotches of color; in their eyes there is no shape or form to the painting, no resemblance to anything they know in real life. If the painter wishes to persuade them he will have to portray some of the things they know

272

and understand, using the familiar things as guaranty of his integrity—even the integrity of his imagination—in portraying also such unexperienced phenomena as wide acres of corn or two-story buildings or, eventually, skyscrapers. In somewhat the same fashion, the dramatist is held to the people—to the people of his day and to the attitudes of his day. (And the fact is not changed if he chooses to set his characters in the shadow of the Tuilleries or upon the plains of Kansas.) He must express his vision of a better day, a nobler race, an ultimate economic security—whatever the "meaning" may be for him—through people and circumstances familiar to his audience. And familiar to the playwright himself.

And he will do it, as it has always been done, more instinctively than deliberately; through creative understanding, which is imagination.

INDEX OF PLAYS, PLAYERS, AND PLAYWRIGHTS

TODAY IN AMERICAN DRAMA